A Place of Sense

A BUR OAK ORIGINAL

Essays in Search of the Midwest

A Place of Sense

Edited by Michael Martone

Photographs by David Plowden

The University of Iowa Press
for the Iowa Humanities Board

University of Iowa Press, Iowa City 52242
Text copyright © 1988 by the Iowa Humanities Board
Photographs copyright © 1988 by David Plowden
All rights reserved
Printed in the United States of America
First edition, 1988
Design by Richard Hendel
Typesetting by G&S Typesetters,
Austin, Texas
Printing and binding by Braun-Brumfield,
Ann Arbor, Michigan

Library of Congress Cataloging-in-Publication Data

A Place of sense: essays in search of the Midwest/edited
   by Michael Martone; photographs by David Plowden.
      p.   cm.—(A Bur oak book)
   Contents: Under the sign of Wonder Bread and Bel-
mont Caskets/Michael J. Rosen—The flatness/Michael
Martone—A writer's sense of place/Louise Erdrich—
The way the country lies/Douglas Bauer—American
Gothic/David Hamilton—If you can talk to a guy/Jane
Staw and Mary Swander—Grandma's backbone,
Dougie's ankles/Gary Comstock—Letting go: the
virtue of vacant ground/Janet Kauffman.
   ISBN 0-87745-211-3.   ISBN 0-87745-217-2 (pbk.)
   1. Middle West—Description and travel.   2. Middle
West—Social life and customs.   I. Martone, Michael.
II. Iowa Humanities Board.   III. Series.
F355.P58   1988   88-15058
977—dc19   CIP

CONTENTS

A Place of Sense

MICHAEL J. ROSEN

Under the Sign
of Wonder Bread and
Belmont Caskets

In January of 1978, I moved to a small island in the
West Indies. I had lived in Columbus, Ohio, for
twenty-six years and had never left or thought of
leaving the country, except for the time in Teen Camp when our
bus passed Buffalo, New York, and we visited a nation distin-
guished solely by the fact that twelve-year-olds could purchase
cherry bombs and bottle rockets four days running in order to re-
linquish them at the American border on the fifth.

Now, for the first time in my life I inhabited a place where
weather was cast into two definite seasons, the wet one and the dry
one. Beyond those major fronts, no forecasts troubled the air-
waves with minor valuations. In the Midwest, thousands of miles
north, the local media had made the transition from news-anchor-
who-also-watched-weather to certified staff meteorologist, and
yet, I could only imagine the weather above the house where I
grew up, cast in Magic Markers and Velcro, its severities ably represented by the drawing of a big umbrella over Mr. Winter's head,
or the adhering of fluffy Colorform—not cumulus—clouds.

My parent's airmail letters confirmed this quaintness. Quite
possibly their handwritings' ingenuousness embodied it. In truth,
I had never read anything my parents had written besides phone
messages or *please-excuse-Michael-from* . . . notes. My father wrote

on memos from his office; my mother, on tissue-weight stationery she must have had printed just to write to me. Yet the contents of their letters converged into a reading of weather and its sidekick, health, as it influenced the local population. Perhaps they assumed it would only make me miss them more were they to report on anything other than the grayish winter in Columbus.

Every part of my lush and arid, foreign surroundings estranged me from the mild suburban life with which I'd been familiar. In the slant of my parents' shy but jocular sentences, Columbus sounded unexceptional and staid. Yet when I told stories from my years in Columbus I detected a different cant, at least in the responses of new friends. Apparently the modest Midwest and my parents as its forecasters, legislators, and developers teetered between an unheard-of sincerity and a heartfelt giddiness.

My first night in the Caribbean was spent in an open-air auditorium with the rest of the island's new residents, learning of the specific dangers of this foreign environment. "Never sleep under manganero trees," the island's minister of health recited. "Their sap is rain-water soluble and caustic." And he continued for an hour: "Don't wear blue jeans in town: They symbolize antigovernment loyalties. . . . Beware of fire coral, sea urchin spines, and barracuda in schools. . . . Never swim at night or alone or anywhere on the south side of the island, where the smell of blood from the slaughterhouse attracts sharks." He also cautioned us about sexual contact with the natives, consuming any form of meat or chicken in the markets, and many other dire and dispiriting facts that fell first into dread, then into disuse, and now into some part of the brain I had once been able to diagram with enormous satisfaction.

But that February, Ohio experienced the severest blizzard within recent memory—even that of my parents'. My father mailed me a picture of my old car's roof barely breaching a four-foot bank of snow, and my mother's head and waving hand frozen in a picture of the snow-blocked picture-window in the dining room. He bought expensive film for the Polaroid he was never comfortable using and sent me a whole portfolio of the neighborhood's month-old abominable snow sculptures that showed no signs of melting. Among those takes, he included a valentine that the new keypunch operator at his office had generated. "The local news," my mother wrote, "is just a list of what's cancelled." My father jotted a few lines about a man in Mansfield, Ohio, who had spent a week marooned in the cab of his truck. And both of them sent clippings about the prayer meeting in the state rotunda, where Governor Rhodes petitioned God to please turn up the world's thermostats.

On Grenada, there were sudden downpours that would drench a sunny, scorching afternoon for two solid minutes, although all signs of rain would evaporate or suck into the dry earth within the next two minutes. I was experiencing the most temperate and personable weather I had ever known. The island flaunted its balmy gifts the way a tourist might, with the gaudiness of pink conches strewn across a black-sand beach, with a wildness of guava, lime, papaya, and coconut trees too accessible not to claim as one's own.

Exempt from Ohio's blizzard, I was not oblivious. During that month I started my own letter-writing binge. I was gathering, in dozens of weekly letters sent mostly to midwestern friends, a new perspective on the place where I had been born and reared, the place I returned to six months later, and the place where I am now living and writing.

When I tried to imagine something more general in which to include my home's geography, I visualized a dittoed worksheet, a lovely smelling blue outline of a heart-shaped state, crazed into eighty-eight fragments. Memorizing the names and whereabouts of each county was our year-long, fifth-grade project. (Eighty-eight was a number just under a million, and it had taken our entire elementary school six months to fill the front-hall showcase with bottlecaps just to help us comprehend the magnitude of that number.)

The year before, we had memorized the capital and location of each state in the United States. The year after that, we made a dent in memorizing the rest of the world's countries before Mrs. Gardner permanently snagged, in its overextended position, the world map, one of the blackboard-size rolls suspended beneath the cursive alphabet. After a spell during which precious board space had been compromised, the custodian removed the whole pedagogical apparatus. Mrs. Gardner intended its return but, from that day forward, our room had no movie screen, no solar system, no topography to show America's ocher rocky parts or the deep-violet swirls of her oceans. Nonetheless each of us had our own country, assigned to us like our own undiscovered heritage.

Our explorations had to include export products and natural resources, but a will toward extra credit supplemented cold facts with warm, almost authentic baked goods the room-mothers heated in the teachers' lounge, hotel brochures with pictures of people swimming outdoors among snow-covered mountains, and multi-colored salt maps.

I was assigned Saskatchewan, a province as foreign to our classroom as Uganda or Samoa. What filled me with enormous pride was the Trip-tik from Columbus to Saskatoon, Saskatchewan, that my parents requisitioned from AAA Motorists Club. I'm sure part of my delight came from the fact that no one else in my class had included such an insert in a report folder's pocket; but part came from the fact that I had received a free tourist's guide, set of road maps, several sight-seeing booklets, and a three-volume, page-by-page, Magic-Marker-highlighted trip to somewhere neither I nor my parents had any intention of ever going.

The fact that I had driven through several other Ohio counties (besides my own, Franklin County) didn't help with the previous year's county quiz, for the relative difference between a county and a country seemed to be held in that lone, additional letter. As for traveling through other states, which we did on our yearly vacation to my aunt's in Massachusetts, I had no vivid sense of anywhere else, any place I could have grown up had my ancestors settled there. I had no real sense of the place in which I *did* grow up. Though I hadn't read Ohioan Louis Bromfield then, I certainly shared his confusion about our state, ". . . the farthest west of the east, and the farthest east of the west, the farthest north of the south, and the farthest south of the north. . . ."

I had seen Ohio and then Ohio and then Ohio regardless of the states passing our windows as we spotted silos and bridges on our Autobingo cards. Even though Columbus boasted that it was "Half-a-Day Away from Half the USA," it took us two days of traveling until we, at last, reached Aunt Renee's.

It has changed slightly since then, but I named the world after people I knew, places that were inconceivable if the homes of relatives hadn't been there, bigger than the dot or the star beside the city's name on the map. So with a child's sense of the world, we children knew that Aunt Renee's meant Massachusetts "near Norman Rockwell's studio"; Great-grandma's meant Florida, "with a swimming pool not twenty feet from the ocean"; and Cedar Point meant an amusement park that featured in everyone's genealogy.

Aside from fourteen-hour trips to Aunt Renee's, the only other traveling we did took twenty minutes or under. It took twenty minutes to reach the kids-under-twelve-pay-what-they-weigh smorgasbord. It took Mother eighteen minutes to drive to whatever shopping mall had just opened. A twenty-five-minute drive delivered us to the Columbus Zoo for a yearly visit with the first gorilla ever born in captivity. For, while our home was located in the midst of Circles and Courts named after a developer's relatives, numerically titled freeways and main streets provided the tangents that could speed us downtown to Lazarus and the Union department stores. These arteries whisked us as easily past the county roads to acres of farmland striped with corn, dotted with cows, basted with the hills and valleys of telephone lines.

We were clearly suburban, something tucked *under* the stature of urban, since ours was one of the first houses built, according to my parents' warnings about tetanus and lockjaw, "in the middle of a rusty barbed-wire cow pasture." What we children understood of this middle-ground between the swelling city and the shrinking country was the lot-by-lot confiscation of the unmowed, grassy fields as our neighbors' houses broke ground, and the gradual disappearance of specimens for the nature center we'd assembled in our two-car garage.

The pleasures of leaving our neighborhood for "a Sunday drive in the country" must have been different for each member of our family, although for all of us, it meant no time limits, destination, or directions. And most importantly, it always meant being with the other four members of our family, in one place, and for a longer interval than our weekly comings and goings sanctioned. The unspoken adventure of the occasion was following unpredicted precipitations—weather, road signage, grumbling stomachs, suggestions from the Sunday paper or someone's recollection or something seen from the car window. I'll concede that my father, the only one of us who knew how to read or correctly refold a road map, might have possessed a greater figure for our wandering.

Thinking of that unwieldy map, I would spread the morning's ready-to-mail letters across my desk in Grenada, sliding the variously shaped envelopes until, fitting against one another, they created the crazed and seceded world of places I loved and missed. I upset my parents when I wrote this in a letter. "We call relatives our roots," I said, "because each person keeps a place from being washed away in our absence."

Snorkling idly, nervously, above a Caribbean—no, an otherworldly—architecture of brain coral and sea fans, I was reminded of the Sunday drive that happened to end at the Blue Hole in Castilia, Ohio, where, through the smeared and scratched glass bottom of a rented boat, we observed bluegill and beer cans swirling in a pit of khaki water. Floating in the Caribbean water, a blue the Blue Hole must have had in a distant part of its collective unconscious, I understood that the actual destination for each drive had been the opportunity to be together, as though family were, itself, a place, and a Sunday drive in the country would bring us there. A definition of my particular Midwest was evolving as a place without definition, as a region that could contain a journey a child might have squiggled across a map.

Our routes would take us along U.S. 40, a road my father maintained stretched clear across the continent like the crack in my salt map of Canada. But how could we believe him, when what we saw of the National Road was a familiar procession of wacky neon and vernacular architecture—the Bambi Lodge, the Robert E. Lee, the *Clean Rooms with Free TV and Telephone*? "Come to Columbus, and Discover America," the city boasted those years, and each motel contributed its farfetched, foreign theme to our singular locale—a colonial inn, a western dude ranch, a tropical paradise, a streamlined 1957 Thunderbird. And yet all was naturalized by the one neon word they shared, "VACANCY," that flashed like a warning light as we zoomed past.

Beyond the motels, and seemingly en route to anywhere we drove, stood Lynn's Fruit Farm, where we drank endless cups of combination ciders, like apple-cherry and pineapple-apple, from dispensers we could work ourselves. Even then I knew the word *spoiled* applied as much to the bushels of bruised apples that would be squeezed in the cider press as it did to my brother, sister, and me, dashing from spigot to spigot, downing as many kinds and cups of cider as it would take to give us a stomachache that evening.

In that same autumn season, the trees importuned my father to pull onto the berm so we could collect leaves from the roadside gully. Somehow they had turned colors we couldn't imagine anywhere but outside our suburb. And yet my father applied the names of trees planted on our new block to these massive, majestic species. We gathered leaf specimens so perfectly edged and colored they announced, like the finding of a four-leaf clover, a quintessence of Nature's power. By a happy coincidence, there were always black walnuts to stain our hands yellow, a grazing horse to feed the sugar cubes that my father produced like a magic trick from his pockets, wrinkled green Osage oranges (large and tropical as anything I could now imagine growing in the Caribbean), and milkweed pods to release from the windows of the moving car in a steam of profligate wishes. Regardless of what we hoarded, Mother could throw out the entire cache before the following Sunday without our noticing, without dimming our enthusiasm for the next week's purveyance.

We passed pottery stands encircled with opalescent strands of reflecting globes, barricaded by towers of flower pots, attended by queues of tiny black jockeys, enraptured St. Francises, and pairs of kissing Dutch children. But most curious to the five of us, driving past the statuary without a single vote to stop and browse, were the herd of deer, the brace of ducks, and the dray of squirrels. Here we were in the country, where, just driving past, we often spotted deer ("Deer X-ing" signs, anyway), usually ducks, and certainly squirrels. But here, too, were houses settled among these creatures—families who set salt licks for the deer, who scattered bread crumbs for the ducks, who shot rock salt at the bulb-digging squirrels—populated with stoneware models of these same creatures nestled in lifelike arrangements in their yards. "Perhaps they attract real ones like decoys," my father hazarded. "Maybe the people still don't spot the real ones *enough*," my mother suggested. "Probably the real animals don't come that close to the house anyway." But once in a while, we sighted real people on their porches and the look on their faces said, "Go ahead and race by, you city slickers. But see how lucky we are to live among all of God's creatures (and, in some niches, even God in the guise of a miniature Virgin Mary or Jesus of the Sacred Heart)."

On the beach near my room in Grenada, a border of unchartered fishing boats hemmed the tame surf into a swimming hole with more fishes than I'd ever seen in all our Sundays of fishing in Ohio. The fishing holes we frequented as a family pooled into a single spot in my memory: the creek on the grounds of a farmer's grazing field across from National Trails Raceway. Oddly, the sound I associate with fishing is not the peace and quiet of cricket wings and cicadas sheltered beneath the soundproof canopy of half-dead trees leaning over a shoreline, but the engine-gunning of funny cars and the indecipherable slur of the broadcast speakers that circled the raceway. We never asked how my father had discovered this amazing fishing hole, or when he had received permission to boost us all over the fence posted "No Trespassing," or why the grazing cattle wouldn't stampede us on our trek to the creek. We trouped across the field with our gear—radio, folding stool, tackle box, comic books, snack sack, wading boots—and set up our afternoon camp.

Once or twice we prepared for the day by setting the car's floor mats on the driveway after a rain to catch nightcrawlers, but usually we bought the bait at a nearby Eskimo Igloo that sold soft ice-cream, licorice-scented doughball, worms, candy bars, and minnows. Worms came in an earth-filled cottage-cheese or Chinesefood takeout container, offering Mother the chance to say, "Who's ready for a little lunch?" giving a couple shakes to the bait.

My father or, to everyone's amusement, my sister would gore a worm on the hooks, and we'd each cast a line into the water, or as often, into the nearby cattails or one another's hair. For the first two minutes, the five of us made a motionless and quiet model of what we imagined the sport required. We could have been a diorama in the Ohio Historical Center, a future scene that might be labeled, "For recreation, Columbus families often journeyed into the wilderness with bamboo poles and primitive carvings of small fishes called 'lures'. . . ." This sustained moment filled my father with a sense of family spirit that must have resembled, in his mind, our hushed and huddled fivesome sitting on the synagogue pew during the High Holy Days. After that initial family frieze, "fishing" had to include roaming the banks for fossils, rummaging through the tackle box, dueling with cattails, skipping shale across the fishing lines, overturning the tackle box, and fighting with one another because, alas, the fluorescent-orange corks and red-and-white bobbers marked the spot from which ripples of boredom issued.

Periodically we checked to see if my father or mother had caught anything and had forgotten to call and show us; *they* checked to see that none of us had fallen in. At different points in the long afternoon, my father would claim to need one of us kids to help him or spell him, and during those returns, a bobber on one of the four or five lines would suddenly sink and rise and flutter—do all the things that our fixed gazes had apparently prevented. We'd grab the pole, reel with the kind of fervor that would either install a backlash in the winding spool or a proud smile on our father's face. He would be leaning with the lowered net as though he expected something that could feed a family of five, and my mother would have jumped up from her folding stool with such excitement that the transistor radio would tumble into the water. And there it would be: a flailing carp, a barbed, chubby catfish, or a slick white bass. Stepping lightly on the fish, my father would pry the hook free, slide a huge pin through its mouth and gills, and, before lowering the stringer of fish into the creek, let us each feel the impossibly heavy heft of the day's catch.

For all our childhood years, my father performed the sport of turning the interminable experience of catching fish into an immediate one. He and Mother kept to themselves the fact that he had caught first the fishes we caught, that he had reeled them in, secured their hooks, and slid each one back into the water, so that the bobber's second dance appeared to his children like a vision of Man and Nature in bounteous harmony.

We didn't need to learn to fish. My father had learned to fish and we had taught him that it was relatively futile to think we could learn anything about lures or the science of flycasting or the virtue of patience. His happiness fell into place beside ours, his wife's, his three children's. When we were old enough to share my father's surefire fishing secret, it was never discussed or declared; he was gone fishing before we had even awakened on Sunday morning— by himself or with an old fishing buddy he had known before his family was born.

This figure of the family featured prominently in the idea of my suburban Midwest as I tendered it in conversations in Grenada, where tonic water is more costly than gin and drinks were mixed in the opposite proportion. Unlike the metropolitan or agrarian or coastal or southern childhoods of my displaced American friends, Columbus provided a place where play and pastime, hobby and happenstance, appeared to be the reigning climate. Experience had no obligation or destiny. Mastery of an activity was seen as an option (another merit badge, a camp elective) rather than a survival skill.

For our family, fishing decidedly did not mean eating fish. We didn't subsist on fish or sell it for our livelihood. Moreover we wouldn't have considered cooking one even for what Mother called "a change of pace." We would go to the drive-in Sunday night and order breaded fish sticks, oblivious to the presence of pound-size bass circling in our trash can/holding tank, or a quartet of carp wrapped in the Sunday paper in the refrigerator's fruit bin. On Monday, my father would give the fish to an appreciative but distant cousin who wouldn't feel obliged to invite us to the feast.

Our other agricultural experiences were likewise limited. Beyond the planting of roses, those delicate annual bushes, my mother's desire for plants of any kind was sated by the dried and dyed bamboo tree that her interior decorator had arranged behind the recovered love seat. The premium concept in market produce wasn't homegrown, but frozen or canned, the remarkable opportunity of the always-on-hand and ready-to-cook. (And canning didn't mean actually immersing vegetables in a boiling water bath; nor did freezing mean a quick blanching and freezing in the garage freezer.) We did have a freezer, for a one-time, supposedly money-saving purchase of half a butchered steer, and the occasional no-limit-per-customer sale on Mountaintop Pies.

I sowed my first garden at the age of twenty. Before that I might have correctly visualized how a carrot grows from the packages in our vegetable bin, and an onion, from the way the ones in our cupboard grew tendrils of green leaves. But the sights of Brussels sprout nodes, a blanching head of cauliflower, or the yellow-blossoming, ground-creeping zucchini were shocks for which nothing in my parents' grassy lot had prepared me.

One year, we did aspire to grow a 350-pound pumpkin from seeds harvested from one of the award-winning giants at the Circle-ville Pumpkin Festival. Throughout the closed-off town square, we had sampled pumpkin in the guise of all of our favorite foods (burgers, waffles, fudge, and milkshakes), and had circled the fenced-in intersection of Circleville that displayed mounds of every kind of shapely and misshapen squash and gourd. Then, just as we were leaving with a crookneck squash as large as my younger sister and a sack of gourds that soon would dry into maracas, my father purchased five of the prize pumpkin's seeds and jotted down the grower's tips for proper cultivation.

That spring we found the seeds in the basement (itself a colossal feat) and sowed them in a bare spot our dog had previously prepared at the back of our yard. Just as the grower had instructed, we predestined the one bloom from all the vines' possible choices to become our prize-winning pumpkin, and committed ourselves to drenching it with five gallons of water every day. Long before it might have reached the 150-pound stage that would have required the roof we had pulled from the dilapidated doghouse to shield it from the sun's rays, our only pumpkin shriveled and rotted. That fall we purchased a manageable, suburb-size pumpkin, carved it into a jack-o'-lantern, and placed it on our porch beside an evergreen in which my father had hidden an old intercom, so that the flame-eyed ghoul could laugh and scream like Vincent Price at all our trick-or-treating friends.

What I understood as my father's ambivalent relationship with the seasons was absent from his well-spaced letters to Grenada. The blizzard so dominated the state that my father was as defenseless as the city's salt truck and snow plow. And once the siege was over, there was only the walk from the driveway to the front door to clear, and even less to write about. His determination typically exhibited itself at critical moments, when fervor would be frustrated by the element at hand. To a child asked to assist, his tasks seemed Sisyphian, even though I didn't know that myth. We shoveled snow when the weatherman predicted six more hours of snow, we raked leaves when the trees were still laden with color, we plucked dandelions when our neighbors' yards were gray with the seed-headed weeds.

During the erratic years our sour-cherry tree chose to bear fruit, we knew it was time for dinner not by the smell of a baking cherry pie, but by the sound of my father's car turning into the driveway, honking at the tree of cherry-robbing starlings. Weren't these the same birds he had fed all winter, trudging across the snow in his fishing boots and bathrobe to refill the suet and seed feeders he'd hung in same cherry tree's boughs?

As children, all our other practice at rural life occurred in day camp. Every summer from the age of four to fourteen, and then for the next ten years as a counselor, I inhabited a wilderness tempered by picnic shelters, nature trails, and capture-the-flag fields. None of these was an overnight camp that involved actually leaving Columbus for some pastoral setting or sports complex. By bus, camp was the typical twenty-minute drive. We encircled our woodsy campsites with burlap and two-by-fours, heated sloppy joes and banana boats on teepee fires we'd built without the benefit of our wadded-up lunchbags, stitched pieces of leather into pocket-comb cases, and took lessons in swimming, archery, canoeing, sailing, and horseback riding.

In Grenada, some friends my own age had never seen a horse more vividly than in pictures, while others had attended riding camps and learned all about English riding and *dressage*. After five years of riding lessons at my camp, I was awarded the much-coveted Pegasus Award, a wallet-size card with a loop of gold ribbon pinned to it. What elevated my riding style from that of the hundred other day campers, I can only guess, for several of us could perform the few requisite maneuvers like distinguishing between clockwise and counterclockwise canters and keeping both hands off the saddlehorn.

Our riding sessions represented the entirety of horse ownership.

Each of us was assigned our lone charge for the four-week session to brush and card, bridle and saddle, feed and water, and then, for an hour, walk, trot, and canter. The stables were an enormous facility with enough horses so that the morning, the afternoon, and the alternate day's campers could each have the responsibility for a horse. And yet, as fierce as our group's commitment, after our four-week session was over, only a few of us returned for the second session, and I don't recall hearing that any of us returned to the stable until the following June, when it appeared that the old stable of horses had been sold and a fresh stable bought.

Just narrating those years of horseback riding on a Caribbean beach cast them into a spoiled and unspoiled light I'd never seen before. On an island where the closest thing to a horse I'd sighted was the donkeys, braided with bougainvillea blossoms, parading in front of the hotels, it dawned on me that hard-mouthed Ranger and spirited Veteran and docile Li'l Lil were all the same Tennessee Walker, and that in each riding class, names were assigned to campers and not to horses. Although the riding instructor used the horse's name when a correction had to be made, weren't we the ones who had made the error, who had recognized the called name, and who would have to hold the reins tighter or squeeze harder with our thighs?

Of all my out-of-the-suburb intervals, horseback riding brought me closest to life-and-death forces. Sure, we had all seen lifeguards towing younger campers from the diving well. My own hands had puffed with poison ivy, my eyes swollen shut. I knew about the danger of heat exhaustion and swallowed the nurse's salt pills when it reached ninety degrees. But nothing had the sting of mortality as the week we had seen, through the bus windows, a dead horse—some camper's, wasn't it?—a horse who had fallen into the creek from the very bridge we were crossing into the stables.

The year after my Pegasus award, my horse Sparky refused my

typical version of neck-reining after a morning in the corral. Later, when we had come to the center of a field, she sank to her knees and slowly rolled onto her side, pinning my leg in the stirrup. A team of adults managed to half-coax and half-pry the immobile horse from my leg. Hysterical, I rode to the tack room hugged between the riding instructor's arms and legs, as she tried to convince me that Sparky would recover from the colic in a week or so. But that was after camp had ended. How would I know? All I could visualize was the sick horse abandoned in the emptied field, as though I had caused whatever "colic" was—my heaviness, the cinch I'd pulled too tight, my child-shaped saddle hugging its heaving chest for dear life.

If it weren't for the challenge of individual achievement, so dramatically different from the teams in which we competed at tent-building, ball games, and paper-bag dramatics, our hours on horseback could be as easily corralled in a letter's paragraph or a mocking aside, as our motley posse was, within the white fence of the stables. Our experience existed safely between earnest horse-assisted work and a pony ride in a shopping center's parked-car corral. And perhaps it is there I detect my first conscious inklings of self-confidence. Despite the presence of instructors, hired hands, and fellow campers, a personal, barely translated relationship existed among a horse, a child, and a rough swatch of the knowable world.

At a distance of thousands of miles, each image from the Midwest, as I held it up for my new friends to consider, looked precious as a souvenir with its locale wood-burned or glittered across it. Qualities sounded like quirks; opportunities, like crazes. I began to worry that anything—an object, a scene, a love—at a distance of memory or miles, must resemble a little photo at the end of a keychain viewer, reduced but enlarged again by the present eye. How could I keep anything I remembered about the Midwest from sounding like a tourist attraction, even an unattractive one? Do we live our lives once as ourselves, then repeatedly as everyone else?

In fact, I could place the scenes and the objects surfacing in my memory of Columbus just opposite the items I was planning to bring back from the island: frond baskets of nutmeg and tumeric (misnamed "saffron") straw embroidered with the words "Spice Island," coconut fudge and coconut tanning oil, unconscionably large bottles of duty-free French colognes, unpunctured conches from six months of culling. Which of them, once I had left the island, would seem anything but garish and sentimental? Is it the ocean I hear in a conch or any breeze to which the ear will fasten a remembered echo?

A tendency to trivialize or tout wasn't something I cultivated. Like any place, when the Midwest became conscious of itself— that it was an original, significant, historical territory—pride set about to mint and market that quality. Such communal recognition requires the additional qualities of kitsch: too much or too many, under- or over-sized, and always in the wrong place. Our family made more than one pilgrimage to Olentangy Indian Caverns, which, whatever else it reported to preserve—frontierism? the wonders of geology?—was a generously brief tour of damp rooms lit by low-wattage bulbs whose theme colors were adapted from the feathered Indian headdresses hung in the gift shop over the plastic arrowheads and beaded belts.

Old MacDonald's Farm might have commemorated our long-standing domestication of livestock; still, we showed our respect by sliding around haylofts, chasing baby goats, and milking cast-concrete cows whose water-filled, rubber udders made perfect squirt guns.

And the Ohio State Fair impersonated every aspect of Ohio's self-consciousness. Just entering the fair through the legs of the H in the thirty-foot-tall "OHIO" admission gates cautioned the visitor that whatever lay ahead was sure to be out of proportion. Something—the August humidity?—had swollen the whole fair, the nation's largest state fair, into near parody of itself. And each booth and building was infected with the same giddiness that came from driving all the way to the state's capital, or the same titilation from viewing Chief, who, at 1,203 pounds, was committed to gaining another 132 pounds to become the world's largest pig.

The fairgrounds woke from its hibernation at the center of a city with a million residents, people who, according to an immense *Reader's Digest* survey in 1958, preferred Westerns and quiz shows above all other television programs (thirteen of the twenty-five most popular). The fair straddled this ambidextrous viewing habit, creating an unofficial body of both kinds of frontierism, a past and a future Midwest, two painted flats with openings for visitors to frame their own faces and be photographed. (Was this another flat—a painting of a headless man at a desk scattered with childhood snapshots—through which I was peering, years later, at my own fair attendance?) Ideology balanced technology, tradition balanced innovation, and nothing balanced the will to excess.

Besides honoring the exceptional in arts such as sheepshearing, corn-relish canning, stoop-masonry, crazy-quilting, and chicken hybridization, the fair featured Ohio's industrial advances. These were highlighted along the midway where, each year, the rides swelled higher, spun faster, ran shorter, and sported longer lines— all technological marvels to a child my age. But the Buckeye Building was the temple of free enterprise, and inside the darkened barn, crowded rows of exhibitors proclaimed that every discovery, of every magnitude, should have a table on which to display its literature, free samples, and register-for-a-free-year's-supply card. Curious, prodigal, peculiar, the displays drew more gasps than the oddities of the sideshow: a space-capsule bank molded before your eyes, a silver cleaner that removed tarnish in one quick dip, a computer-generated personality analysis.

The move from Columbus to the West Indies focused this midwestern integration. In Grenada, the primitive abutted the progressive, native heritage against modern heresy. The only harmony I could detect appeared to be the afternoon hour when no one worked. Although there were no dairy cows on the island to spark it, a vivid memory of mine featured the Ohio State Fair's particular combination of country craft and scientific advance: the butter sculptures inside Dairy Barn. Since the early nineteen-hundreds, one of three men has sculpted nearly half a ton of fresh butter into the shape of a cow. Since I can remember, the exhibit has always included the cow, her calf, and a featured third figure to reflect a contemporary theme. What began as a modest culinary whim—the molding of a butter pat into a curlicue or flower—has become a seasonal occupation, predicated on the impulse to combine the staple with the caprice into an artistic medium for popular culture. Annually, the sculptors transformed Ohio's own butter into Ohio boys like Bob Hope, Coach Woody Hayes, racecar driver Bobby Rayhall, Jack Nicklaus, and Neil Armstrong (waving a flag on a moonscape made of butter—*not* green cheese), into the non-Ohioan Darth Vader, and into a butter child in a wheelchair, reaching for a butter butterfly that dangles out of reach.

At dinners in the school cafeteria, I laughed with my Caribbean friends as I described the sculptures I had seen. The paradoxical combination seemed as oddly conceived as the dessert the native cooks had prepared especially for us Americans: gelled imported Jello (primarily a protein) dissolving around chunks of indigenous papaya (containing an enzyme that breaks down protein). But the humor had the glow of homage. And didn't it sound vaguely holy for a man to create a cow from the very butter the man had created from the cow?

Michael J. Rosen   19

If it wasn't holiness or wholesomeness, perhaps it was just the spirit of adventure that gave such added license to the spirit of Columbus entrepreneurs. Certainly the most common form had already taken hold—the way gardeners say certain weeds take hold—on the lawns in our own neighborhoods: houses that existed in a state of perpetual garage, yard, and tag sale. (A mild biennial form had even attacked my mother and her friends. Indeed, the first profit I had ever "made" came from contributing things my parents had bought me or I had bought with my allowance to our garage sale.)

Nearby homes expressed their commercial aspirations by hanging a "Beauty Parlor Supplies" or a "Dogs Groomed" sign in what was clearly a dining-room window. More extenuated longings in Columbus founded multiple-business establishments. Our city preserved the idea of "both," as though a midwestern career choice meant heads and tails, and even multiples of each. We frequently passed Kennedy's, a single facade labeled in huge block letters: MARINE ACCESSORIES, FISHING SUPPLIES, HUNTING GEAR, CAKE DECORATING. Another neighborhood enjoyed the convenience of the Glorious Corner, an ex-gas-station offering its services as a Revival-Hall/Soft-Serve-Ice-Cream-Stand/Thrift Shop/Dry Cleaners. An easy drive away stood Odero Sinoh's, a Beverage Drive-Through/Party Mart/Lounge/Auto-Leasing Company. What other service could a neighborhood require?

Before my birth in Columbus, that same imagination created Big Bear, the nation's first supermarket. Alas, I was born decades too late to see the trained bear lumbering along the (then) strangely accessible aisles, pawing particular comestibles into a cart, thereby testifying to the ease of *going* shopping. That mindset spawned Town and Country, the nation's first shopping center, a stretch of individual businesses that offered, more than windows decorated with the latest goods, a vision of the future. And that heady will-to-patronize established Columbus as an official All-American City, which meant that in the minds of corporate and commercial ventures, we were the ideal headquarters, test market, and trial base. Fast-food chains like White Castle, Wendy's, and Rax began their successes with people I knew, perhaps even with my own mother, who would meet me outside the school cafeteria with an enviable hot lunch from Wendy's.

I hadn't realized the extent of my own immersion in commercial testing until I learned that my Caribbean acquaintances had never consumed a childhood cereal of sugary flakes and dehydrated bits of ice cream. They had never purchased chocolate- or vanilla-flavored gum as we had for an enthusiastic but unrepeated chew. Flubber, that purple cube of wiggly plastic that appeared at Kiddie Korner just after Fred MacMurray's success in *The Absent-Minded Professor*, was never found in their living-room carpeting or sibling's hair along with Silly Putty and Goop—nor in their trash cans when, a month later, Flubber was withdrawn from the market for causing rashes.

Would Americans buy film from a shed-size ladybug settled in a pizza parlor's parking lot? Would families use a toilet paper roll that released a rose fragrance when a sheet was torn free? Would mothers prefer Coca-Cola in a family-size jug? Would husbands buy more Stroh's beer if the can was white instead of gold? If a corporation wanted to know the answers, people just like my family, living in Columbus, Ohio, could tell them. Our size, our age, ethnic and income distribution represented the nation as a whole— we *were* the All-American City.

My first authentic glimpse of industry was our school visit to a commercial bakery. Downtown, the aroma of baking bread was as pronounced as the looming letters of "WONDER BREAD" that rose, one glowing red word over the other, above the adjacent neighborhood. Most of the time we could see only the one word

Michael J. Rosen   21

"WONDER" revealed between the blockade of downtown silhouettes. At night, the word loomed beside the other prominent white factory lights that proclaimed "BELMONT CASKETS."As far as I knew, Columbus produced bread and coffins, the slices that covered the cheese and tomatoes packed in my school lunch, and the tombs that Boris Karloff and Bela Lugosi occupied every Saturday afternoon during a triple horror feature. Together, those two large, legible phrases of the skyline extended the city's hospitable greetings—or was it a warning?—to travelers on the downtown freeways.

The Wonder Bread factory, the very place that baked the bread which helped our bodies grow in twelve essential ways, created a flush of excitement second only to the Invisible Woman and her series of illuminated organs at the Center for Science and Industry, our other school field trip. "Overly refined," "mass produced," "preservatives," "unwholesomeness"—not a negative quality entered our minds or our tour, for by the end of our visit we had possession of a food more miraculous than manna: the identical family-size loaf transformed into a miniature loaf each of us could take, just for visiting. As it happened, those precious slices of white bread molded before I'd let my mother profane two pieces in a sandwich.

This was the time period when marketing strategies, packaging, premiums, and associated entertainment eclipsed their own commodities. Before becoming a writer with the occupation's typically attendant obsessions, my favorite mail was the small sample package. It didn't matter if the product tucked inside was non-spotting dishwasher detergent, creamier hand cream, secretly disguised sanitary napkins, or country-fresh air freshener—each was special because it was improved, new, or advanced; unannounced, free, and miniature; and because *you couldn't buy it at the store even if you wanted to!* How had we been singled out to deserve these treats? And what could we do to get more? The samples had been sent to us just for living where we lived, on Bolton Avenue, in Columbus, Ohio.

With a vividness that borders on permanent damage, I can recall the thin, squishable packets of Herbal Essence Shampoo that arrived frequently enough that my mother never needed to purchase a bottle. These were the years when the peace symbol, spray-painted on overpasses and bathroom walls, was never mistaken for the Mercedes-Benz logo, and our late awakening to ecology urged us to compensate by rinsing our hair with scents from the green world.

Correspondingly, our family meals found inspiration in invention. "Freeze-dried," "evaporated," "instant," and "condensed" became the essential catch-phrase qualities, just as "vitamin-enriched" and "like Grandma used to make" had been for previous generations, and swayed Mother toward purchases much more frequently than did our taste buds. We children relished the idea of TV dinners, particularly if we could eat them on TV trays while watching "Peter Pan" or "Soupy Sales" on TV. To witness the cooking of a boil-in-a-bag dinner provided an evening's sustenance. The thrill of whacking the dinner rolls' cardboard tube on the edge of the new Formica eclipsed the sensual experience of warm, aromatic bread.

Something probably went caterwaul in our sense of appreciation, but pleasures no longer issued from the simple consumption of something wonderful, but from its convenience or novelty or a tangential prize or contest. Real value in a purchase was determined by what other thing was thrown in, redeemable, or discounted. Our glassware came from fill-ups at the gas station, our dish towels from jumbo boxes of detergent, our toaster-oven by changing banks, our toys inside or on cereal boxes, our walkie-talkies and electric carving knife from pasting grocery stamps into little booklets.

We were real, hard-working, sincere, prospering people entitled

Michael J. Rosen 23

to these real values. And by virtue of this, we could win incredible things. In fact, according to the posters at the drugstore and the letters in our mailbox, we might already be winners. Disc jockeys were combing the city at random, ready to give prizes to our license plate! All we'd have to do is pick up the phone and call. The host of "Bowling for Dollars" telephoned someone in our area every Saturday afternoon with dinners-for-two at restaurants with table-side cooking. And if we hadn't registered, sent in a postcard with our names, or filled out an entry blank, we could always identify with the winners. They were people like us. An afternoon with the flu, and I watched contestants on "Supermarket Sweep" running down the aisle of a store just like our Big Bear, raking the tinned hams and cigarette cartons into their shopping carts just like the bear himself. I watched the women on "Queen for a Day" receive all the unaffordable things like Oneida silverware, and a new electric clothes dryer, and even a certificate from the Spiegel catalog. People from Ohio were on that program; they had even filmed a week's episode at Veterans Memorial Auditorium, where my parents had taken me to a concert by the Supremes *with* Diana Ross. But beyond actual participation, I could hear, in round after round, a list of personal tragedies that far exceeded anything I'd ever experienced, and I could hold an elbow in one hand and use my other forearm like the applause meter that appeared on the screen, measuring, for myself, each heartbreaking, disaster-ridden, poverty-stricken degree of desperation. And then I could feel the glut of prizes, heavy as the queen's crown and cape and armload of roses, smothering any residual grief beneath its weight. By the time "Flippo, the Clown," was broadcast, I had watched "Let's Make a Deal," "The Price Is Right," and "The Newlywed Game," and the things we didn't own, the answers and tragedies and opportunities I didn't possess, occupied my bedroom like the germs that were keeping me home from school.

We cherished the experience of icing cupcakes with ready-to-spread canned frosting, withdrawing money from a sliding drawer at a drive-through teller, and borrowing books from a green bus that pulled into the school playground once a month. Between a pair of panning searchlights, we shopped for cars in lots occupied with barbecues, a hot-air balloonist, midget clowns, and a woman frozen in a block of ice. Supermarkets solicited our attention by inviting an amusement park to settle in front of their doors. Which store for new school shoes? The ones where we could receive the next in the series of Buster Brown toys and our parents could peek into a small step-up X-ray machine with no foresight into radiation's dangers, and confirm how snugly their babies' feet fit inside the booties they had selected. An innocence was applied, like an unconditional guarantee, to anything advanced. And Columbus appeared to be as advanced as any place in the world.

This minor, applied technology was a second point of perspective through which I could imagine the Midwest. Further comparison with Grenada brought an overlooked poignancy to the trials and tests "suffered" by Columbus families. On the island, labor was the age-old, time-tested product, and could be purchased for fewer East Caribbean Dollars than batteries or spray starch. Most American students easily afforded someone to garden, iron, shop, cook, clean, and drive.

The demonstrations I experienced as a child had nothing to do with rebellious blue jeans and civil rights, although Columbus had made little enough progress in that area. Our attentions were trained on domestic demonstrations. To witness was to want. "Try our new smokey cheese on a cracker?" a woman just like my mother would ask, piping an orange stream from the nozzle of an inverted can. Was she the same Ohio housewife who had never dreamed of being in a commercial but said OK to this one because her family truly preferred this brand above the others? Crepe-paper streamers waving in an air conditioner's breeze, a fried egg sliding from a hot skillet sprayed with PAM—these fascinated us children the way movie stars did our parents' generation. What could be more enchanting than watching an appliance perform a herculean labor like vacuuming a clear path in a pile of spilled straight pins. Comparatively it was an easy task to imagine how it might smooth the dents of our footprints on Mother's new shag.

My desired but never-acquired favorite was a blender—an Osterizer, I think—that must have had the sound of a tree chipper, although no one would notice this at the time of purchase amid the general din of the Buckeye Building. I hadn't imagined what use our family would have for the powerful machine, but I *had* sampled a strawberry milkshake concocted from egg shells, celery, and beets poured by the smiling man into the same kind of tiny cup from which I had drunk my "Don't Forget Sabin on Sunday" polio vaccine. *Indispensable*, I remember the aproned man saying into the microphone around his neck. "But it's indispensable," I implored my mother, feeling the kitchen of our new house grow steadily outdated and outmoded. How had she resisted the knife we'd seen together the previous day at the fair, the one that glided through a brick-hard package of frozen spinach and diced whole onions in a few deft strokes? "The only tears you'll cry are tears of joy," the demonstrator promised. Was it our imagination or our conscience that took a cue from an onion's ability to draw tears? We trained ourselves not to look away but to look forward, forward to owning such aids to modern living.

At my desk in Grenada, I wanted the objects and experiences I was recovering—in letters, conversations, and revisions of memory—to remain independent and intact. Yet I knew I couldn't help but do as the word *recover* implied: hide each one again beneath memory, even beneath the memory of a memory. The danger with the things that recollection has chosen is their willfulness.

Deserving or not, each hopes to be a symbol—at the least, a symbol of what we've forgotten.

At a desk now, in Columbus, Ohio, I have hoped that my recollections of Grenada and the Midwest I began to describe there would resist similar tidiness. Is it possible to see the native and the derived qualities, the species and the spectacles, that formed some version of a midwestern sensibility as opposing only in the way magnetic poles oppose, creating a force that suspends each charged item between the values of its field?

It *is* tempting to say: My reason for leaving Columbus was to be a physician *and* a writer; my reason for returning to Columbus, to be a writer. But what is so reasonable about a single reason?

I had enrolled in a medical school with students who, shunted along an uncertain foreign route, possessed a singular determination: to pass the entrance exam into an American medical school. Unlike my colleagues, I subsisted on British novels, composing letters, journal writing, and toying with images for poems and my first stories. In a far-too-conscious part of my mind, there was a compound image of myself: family physician by day, writer at night, with the additional hope that one vocation's hours would illuminate the others. "The choices are yours," replayed in my head. "Whatever makes you happy will make us happy." Weren't those the voices of a test-market city, a free sample of midwestern indulgence, a personal challenge to go where no one I knew had gone before?

I left Grenada in late May with the rest of the medical school. The rainy season was beginning. In Columbus the weather service announced a high-pressure system and unseasonable warmth. I wrote St. George's School of Medicine for a leave of absence. That summer I made the decision not to be a doctor and, at that point, not to be a writer necessarily, but to begin doing things writers did. Columbus, in the person of my parents, greeted this

Michael J. Rosen 27

decision with the same open arms that had embraced the idea of my being a doctor and had annually embraced a child's fickle experiments and fascinations. I'd like to hold them open there, if I could. I'd like to hold all of my suburban Midwest in a similarly open gesture of encouragement, discovery, and watchfulness, and think of myself, now, as a combination butter sculptor/pumpkin grower/part-owner of an Appaloosa named Pegasus, minding my own small business under the sign of Wonder Bread and Belmont Caskets.

The Flatness

They are thinking about northern Ohio, about Indiana, about the long stretch through Illinois and on into Iowa. It is flat. The geometry of the fields suggests a map as large as the thing it represents. The squared township roads score the axes of coordinates. The cusp of trees on the horizon, the water tower, the elevator are tokens slid there representing ground taken and held. The only dimension marked by Z is the state of dreaming as they drive on the interstates meandering in tangents that seek what the railroads, who were here with rulers first, called a water-level route.

There are places in the Midwest that are not like this—the limestone hills, the loess bluffs, the forest lakes and sand dunes, the rills and knobs and kettles. But the people who know the place only by driving through it know the flatness. They skim along a grade of least resistance. The interstate defeats their best intentions. I see them starting out, big-hearted and romantic, from the density and the variety of the East to see just how big this country is. They are well read, and they have a vision as they come out of the green hills and the vista opens up, a true vision so vast that at night as they drive there are only the farmyard lights that demonstrate plane geometry by their rearranging patterns. And, in the dawn around Sandusky, they have had enough, and they hunker down and drive, looking for the mountains that they know are ahead somewhere. They cannot see what is all around them now. A kind of blindness afflicts them, a pathology of the path. The flatness.

It *is* flat. I grew up on a plain scoured by four or five glaciers that once was the floor of a shallow inland sea. On the interstate, when I drove from Fort Wayne to Indianapolis the overpasses scaled above the county roads and railways. On either side of the ascending ramp little right-triangle lakes glistened. The holes, now topped with water, provided the fill for the overpass ramps, illustrating some law of conservation that you can go only as high as you go deep. From the artificial vantage of these overpasses I could see, yes, for miles to the islands of trees or yawing barn, a house on a reach. And way off in the distance, the land almost met the paralleling sky, the flat-bottomed clouds, and there between the land and clouds hung a strip of air without color that the sun set through.

It is flat for the people who drive through, but those who live here begin to sense a slight unevenness. As I drove down the perfectly straight highway, I waited for the gentle natural rise, no overpass, like taking off in a jet, before the steep climb, the moment the front wheels of the plane leave the ground. And then I'd drop back down and cross a bridge over a river, the Wabash, the Salamonie, or the Mississinewa. The bump had been the end moraine of a glacier. The river is still in place from the melting and washout. These ridges are scalloped together in the plain like tide lines on the beach, a few extra grains of sand. I know it isn't much, the highlight of a road trip a slight elevation that could be missed if you were fiddling with the radio dial. But to such a scale has my meter been calibrated. Living in a flat country, I began to read the flatness, to feel the slight disturbances in the field, to drive over it by the seat of my pants.

And on that plain where I grew up, there is a continental divide. Unlike the more famous one in the Rockies, in Indiana it is a matter of a few feet. Two rivers meet in the city of Fort Wayne, and the third one they form flows back on the tributaries. It looks strange on a flat map, like a dual-lane highway. The new river heads back north and east, paralleling its headwaters going the other way. Rain falling on the east side of Fort Wayne eventually finds its way to the Atlantic. On the west, the rain will fall and travel to the Gulf of Mexico. It is a matter of a few feet. I tried to imagine continental watersheds sloping away from me. I lived in a neighborhood called North Highlands. Before the developers came up with that name it was known as Hungry Hill because once during winter the horse drays couldn't climb the icy slopes with food. It isn't much of a hill, but it is another ending of a glacier. It is just high enough so that it is the only part of town that never floods. Since I've been alive, Fort Wayne has had three hundred-year floods, floods that are supposed to happen only once a century. The flooding is due to the flatness. After a heavy rain or a good snow melt, water everywhere starts to rise, in the rivers and ditches. It pools in sheets from the saturated ground. It can't run off since the ground is so level, so it rises. There is a skim of water in the streets. The parks are lakes. The flooding is gradual. Often it takes days. The water is finding the balance, finding the contour that runs through the town like a fault before it moves. The water keeps rising and spreading. The water, never running very fast in the river beds, stops altogether now, quivers at the brim of the old levees like that lip of water, a couple of molecules thick, that shimmers above the rim of a full glass. Fort Wayne floods are slow disasters, with people going to work as usual while others pump their basements or fill sandbags. There is always plenty of warning. There is always nothing to be done. There is not much raging water. Homes are inundated at the same speed it takes to repaint them. And when the owners repaint the houses, they dash a little line on the doorsill to mark the high water of this flood.

The flatness informs the writing of the Midwest. The flatness of the landscape can serve as a foil, the writing standing out, a kind of

Blue Hotel, in opposition to the background. There is enough magical realism to go around here. A friend, Michael Wilkerson, goes so far as to call the Indiana Toll Road the Bermuda Triangle of Highway Travel. It's true. People who drive through have stories. They report mysterious breakdowns, extradimensional rest stops, and miraculous appearances of state troopers. In the whiteout of the passage through the flatness, dreaming can take over. The dull colors richen. The corn in the fields begins to sparkle like the cellophane corn on the set of the *Wizard of Oz*. And that movie, with its *film noir* depiction of the Midwest, suggests another way of capturing this place.

I can still remember Danny Kaye introducing the movie on TV, telling the kids not to worry, that the black and white of Kansas was just the way they made the picture. Then as now, those grays of the monotonous landscape interested me more than the extravagant color. I have my mirages but they are nothing fancy—the mirror of water that coats the hot road ahead reflects the flat sky and galvanizes the horizons. For me this Midwest is the perfect setting, this matter of a few degrees, a few feet either way. Here is ground that turns at once into swamp then into sea, each a solid calm surface, beneath them all a slight tilt, a tendency really, a bias so subtle you never notice that you've crossed a line, that you've reached a crisis, that your whole world has changed.

I dislike the metaphor of the Heartland. True, the Midwest is somewhere near the physical center of the map of America. But the Heartland implies that, here at some exact center, lies something secret, hidden and important, an X for a buried treasure. The Midwest is too big to be seen like that. I think of it more as a web of tissue, a membrane, a skin. And the way I feel about the Midwest is the way my skin feels and the way I feel my own skin—in layers and broad stripes and shades, in planes and in the periphery. The Midwest as hide, an organ of sense and not power, delicate and coarse at the same time. The Midwest transmits in fields and waves. It is the place of sense. It sometimes differentiates heat and cold, pain and pleasure, but most often registers the constant bombardment, the monotonous feel of feeling. Living here on the great flat plain teaches you a soft touch, since sensation arrives in huge sheets, stretched tight, layer upon layer, another kind of flood.

Perhaps I make too much of geology, topography imprinting on our lives. It was the Romantics of the last century who gave us mountains as something beautiful to see instead of as impediments to get over. From them too we have inherited "the view." I grew up in a landscape not often painted or photographed. The place is more like the materials of the art itself—the stretched canvas and paper. The midwestern landscape is abstract, and our response to the geology of the region might be similar to our response to the contemporary walls of paint in the museums. We are forced to live in our eyes, in the outposts of our consciousness, the borders of our being. Forget the heart. In the flatness, everywhere is surface. This landscape can never take us emotionally in the way smokey crags or crawling oceans can. We stare back at it. Beneath our skins, we begin to disassemble the mechanisms of how we feel. We begin to feel.

LOUISE ERDRICH

A Writer's Sense of Place

In a tribal view of the world, where one place has been inhabited for generations, the landscape becomes enlivened by a sense of group and family history. Unlike most contemporary writers, a traditional storyteller fixes listeners in an unchanging landscape combined of myth and reality. People and place are inseparable. The Tewa Pueblo, for example, begin their story underground, in complete darkness. When a mole comes to visit, they learn there is another world above and decide to go there. In this new place the light is so intense that they put their hands over their eyes to shield them. Grandmother Spider suggests that they adjust their vision to the light by gradually removing their hands and she points them to Sandia Mountain, the place where they will live. A great deal of wandering, bickering, lessons learned, and even bloodshed occur, but once there, they stay for good.

This is the plot but not the story. For its full meaning, it should be heard in the Tewa language and understood within that culture's world view. Each place would then have personal and communal connotations. At the telling of it we would be comfortable, old friends. Our children would be sleeping or playing nearby. Old people would nod when parts were told the right way. It would be a new story and an old story, a personal story and a collective story, to each of us listening.

What then of those nonindigenous to this land? In renaming and historicizing our landscapes, cityscapes, towns, and neighborhoods, writers from Hawthorne to Cather to Faulkner have attempted to weld themselves and their readers closer to the new world. As Alfred Kazin notes in *On Native Grounds*, "The greatest single fact about our American writing . . . [is] our writers' absorption in every last detail of this American world, together with their deep and subtle alienation from it."

In some instances, this is also true for contemporary Native American writers. The narrator of James Welch's terse *Winter in the Blood* reflects, "Coming home was not easy anymore. It was never a cinch, but it had become a torture. My throat ached, my bad knee ached, and my head ached in the even heat. . . . It could have been the country, the burnt prairie beneath a blazing sun, the pale green of the Milk River valley, the milky waters of the river, the sagebrush and cottonwoods, the dry, cracked gumbo flats. The country had created a distance as deep as it was empty, and people accepted and treated each other with distance."

Perhaps this alienation is the result of one difficult fact about the dominant culture, from which Welch's narrator returns at the beginning of the story—its mutability, its basis in progressive movement. Nothing, not even the land, can be counted on to stay the same. And for the writers I've mentioned, and others, it is therefore as if, in the very act of naming and describing what they love, they lose it.

Faulkner's story "The Bear" is set in "that doomed wilderness where edges were being constantly and punily gnawed at by men with plows and axes who feared it because it was wilderness." That shrinking area is haunted by a spirit, the bear, which is "shaggy, tremendous, red-eyed, not malevolent but just big, too big for the dogs which tried to bay it, for the horses which tried to ride it down, for the men and the bullets they fired into it; too big for the very country which was its constricting scope."

To Europeans, the American continent was so vast that only a few hundred years ago it seemed that nothing and no one could ever truly affect it. Yet William Faulkner wrote nostalgically of a wilderness that had already vanished. What Faulkner invents, and laments, is the spread of space that was lost piecemeal to agriculture. The great bear, which is the brooding and immense spirit of the land, had all but disappeared from settled areas before Faulkner was born and exists today largely by virtue of human efforts on its behalf. The wilderness that once claimed us is now claimed and consumed by us. Carefully designated scraps of it are kept increasingly less pristine to remind us of what was.

Just as Faulkner laments the passing of the Southern forests into farmland, so Willa Cather's novels about Nebraska homesteaders are elegies to vanishing virtues, which she links with an unmechanized and pastoral version of agriculture. That view has been giving way ever since as developments in chemical fertilizers, hybrid seed, animal steroids, and farm equipment become part of a more technological treatment of the land.

Douglas Unger's novel, *Leaving the Land*, tells of the rise and fall of a small town in South Dakota that bases its economy on large-scale turkey farming. When prices fall and the farmers can't afford to ship their stock, they slaughter the turkeys, pile them in a trench, and burn them. Unger writes of the unlikely, apocalyptic scene, "The prairie filled with black smoke whirling up day after day, rolling, tumbling, dark scarves of smoke blown for an instant to the shapes of godheads, vague monuments, black smoke tornadoes that scarred the summer skies with waste and violence."

Instead of viewing a stable world, as in pre-invasion Native American cultures, instead of establishing a particular historical background for the landscape, American writers seem bound into the process of chronicling change and forecasting destruction, of recording a world before that world's very physical being shifts.

As we know, neighborhoods are leveled in a day. The Army Corps of Engineers may change the course of a river. In the ultimate kitsch gesture of a culture's desperation to engrave itself upon an alien landscape, a limestone mountain may be blasted into the likenesses of important men.

Suburbs and suburban life may be monuments as representative as Mount Rushmore. There is a boring grandeur to the acres on acres of uniform cul-de-sacs, wide treeless streets, green yards adorned by pools that sparkle like blue opal. The larger malls are awe-inspiring Xanadus of empty opulence. Although created as escapes, as places halfway between country and city life, but without the isolation of the one or the crime of the other, suburbs and the small-town way of life they imitate are often, in our literature, places to escape from. One departs either back to the evil thrills, pace, and pollution of the city, or to the country, where life is supposedly more deeply felt, where the people are supposedly more genuine, where place is idiosyncratic and not uniform. For the only American writers whose "old country" exists within the boundaries of the United States, departure from the city or surburbia is a complex affair, for it means returning to the reservation.

As the Laguna Pueblo/Sioux writer Paula Gunn Allen writes in *The Sacred Hoop*, "A tribal member's estrangement from the web of tribal being and the conflict that arises are the central preoccupations of much of contemporary American Indian literature." Returning to the design of Montana reservation life, the narrator Christine, in Michael Dorris's *A Yellow Raft in Blue Water*, is beset with contradictions that resolve in a moment of transcendence. Christine is dying, but for the first time in her life, she is also content to be still, to be a part of and not the center of the world. She sits down. "The evening wasn't cool yet, but it would be, and I didn't plan to move again. As the night deepened, the wire mesh became invisible, a passage opening into a lighter blackness, and before my eyes the stars lit. They were the windows of a faraway city. They were the points of silver nails pressing through tar paper. They were a field of glowbugs, motionless in time."

Of course not every writer feels compelled to particularize or unite with his or her setting. Samuel Beckett, Alain Robbe-Grillet, Nathalie Saurrette, and Donald Barthelme are a few writers whose work could take place anywhere, or nowhere. Gerald Vizenor, the Anishinabe writer, places his characters both in a specific tribal setting and out, in a labyrinth of wordplay and intercultural magic. Since in contemporary American society mobility is characteristic of our experience, most of us don't grow up in one place anymore, and even if we do we are usually required by convention to leave it. How many of us live around the corner from parents, grandparents, even brothers and sisters? How many of us come to know a place deeply, over generations? How many places even exist that long? We are part of a societal ebb and flow, a people washing in and out of suburbs and cities. We move with unparalleled ease, assisted by Mayflower Van Lines and super-highways. We are nomadic, both by choice, relocating in surroundings that please us, and more often by necessity. Like hunter-gatherers, we must go where we will be fed, where the jobs are listed.

But if for many readers and writers place is not all-important, there still remains the problem of identity and reference. A writer needs for his or her characters to have something in common with the reader.

If not the land, which changes, if not a shared sense of place, what is it then that currently gives us a cultural identity? What is it that writers may call on now for common references in the way that a Tewa could mention Sandia Mountain?

Whether we like it or not, we are bound together by that which may be cheapest and ugliest in our culture, but may also have an austere and resonant beauty in its economy of meaning. We are bound by common references to mass culture, to the brand names of objects, to symbols like the golden arches, to stories of folk heroes like Ted Turner and Colonel Sanders, to entrepreneurs of comforts that cater to our mobility like Conrad Hilton and Leona Helmsley. These symbols and heroes may annoy us, or comfort us, when we encounter them in literature; at the very least they give us context.

It means one thing for a character to order an imported Heineken beer in a story, another thing for that person to order a Schlitz. There is a difference in what we perceive in that character's class and sensibility. It means a third thing for that person to order a Hamm's beer, reputed to be made of Minnesota's sky-blue waters, often the brew of choice for Jim Northrup's Chippewa. Brand names and objects in fiction connote class, upbringing, aspirations, even regional background. Very few North Dakotans drive Volvos, even though quite a few North Dakotans are of Swedish descent. The Trans-Am is not the car of choice for most professors of English in eastern colleges. The characters in *Winter in the Blood* drive troublesome old John Deeres.

In Bobby Ann Mason's stories, characters drink bourbon and Coke out of coffee cups, while the people in Robb Forman Dew's novels use pitchers for milk instead of pouring it from cartons, and transfer jam from jars to crystal dishes. Raymond Carver's characters drink Teachers', nameless gins, or cheap pink champagne. Few of Eudora Welty's characters drink that sort of thing, while some of William Kennedy's characters would be happy to get it.

Though generalized, these examples show the intricacies of our cultural shorthand. And if it seems meaningless or vulgar to cling to and even celebrate the trash that inundates us, consider our culture without McDonald's or the home computer, a prospect that would be possible only in the event of some vast and terrible catastrophe.

We live with the threat of nuclear obliteration, and perhaps this is a subliminal reason that as writers we catalog streets, describe landmarks, create even our most imaginary landscapes as thoroughly as we can. No matter how monotonous our suburbs, no matter how noxious our unzoned Miracle Miles and shopping centers, every inch would seem infinitely precious were it to disappear.

In her essay "Place in Fiction," Eudora Welty speculates that the loss of place might also mean the loss of our ability to respond humanly to anything. She writes: "It is only too easy to conceive that a bomb that could destroy all trace of places as we know them, in life and through books, could also destroy all feelings as we know them, so irretrievably and so happily are recognition, memory, history, valor, love, all the instincts of poetry and praise, worship and endeavor, bound up in place."

I don't know whether this is true. I hope that it is not, and that humanity springs from us and not only from our surroundings. I hope that even in the unimaginable absence of all place as we know it something of our better selves would survive.

But the danger that they wouldn't, we wouldn't, that nothing else would either, is real and present. Leonard Lutwak urges, in his book *The Role of Place in Literature*, that this very fear should inform the work of contemporary writers and act as a tool to further the preservation of the earth. "An increased sensitivity to place seems to be required," he says, "a sensitivity inspired by aesthetic as well as ecological values, imaginative as well as functional needs. It may be concluded that literature must now be seen in terms of the contemporary concern for survival."

In our worst nightmares, all of us have imagined what the world might be like *afterward* and have feared that even the most extreme versions of a devastated planet are not extreme enough. Consider, then, that to Native Americans it is as if the unthinkable has happened, and relatively recently. Many Native American cultures were destroyed more thoroughly than even a nuclear disaster might destroy ours, and others live on with the fallout of that destruction, effects persistent as radiation—poverty, fetal alcohol syndrome, chronic despair.

Through diseases such as measles and smallpox, and a policy of cultural extermination, the population of Native North American inhabitants shrank from an estimated fifteen million in the mid-fifteenth century, to just over 200,000 by 1910. That is proportionately as if the population of the United States were to decrease from its present level to the population of Cleveland. Entire pre-Columbian cities were wiped out, different linguistic and ethnic groups eliminated. Since the ravages of disease preceded even the first explorers, the full magnificence and variety of Native American cultures were never chronicled, perceived, or known by Europeans.

Contemporary Native American writers have before them a task quite different from that of non-Indian writers. In the light of enormous loss, they must tell the untold stories of contemporary survivors, while protecting and celebrating the cores of cultures left in the wake of the European invasion.

And yet, in this, there always remains the land. The approximately 3 percent of the United States that is still held by Native American nations is cherished in each detail, still lit with old tribal myths, still known and used, in some cases, changelessly. It is arduous, it is difficult to come home, but the Acoma Pueblo poet Simon Ortiz writes of return with hope.

> Survival, I know how this way.
> This way, I know.
> It rains.

Mountains and canyons and plants
grow.
We travelled this way,
gauged our distance by stories
and loved our children.
We taught them
to love their births.
We told ourselves over and over
again, "We shall survive
this way."

All of this brings me, at last, to try and describe what a sense of place means from my own perspective.

I grew up in a small North Dakota town, on land which once belonged to the Wahpeton-Sisseton Sioux but had long since been leased out and sold to non-Indian farmers. Our family of nine lived on the very edge of town, in a house that belonged to the government and was used to house employees of the Bureau of Indian Affairs boarding school, where both of my parents worked, and where my grandfather, a Turtle Mountain Chippewa named Pat Gourneau, had been educated. The campus consisted of an immense central playground, a school building, two dormitories, as well as numerous outbuildings. All of these places were made of a kind of crumbly dark red local brick. When cracked, smashed, or chipped back to clay, this brick gave off a peculiar, dry, choking dust that I can almost still taste.

On its northern and western sides, the campus ran, with no interference from trees or fencelines, into fields of corn, wheat, soybeans, or flax. I could walk for miles down perfectly straight dirt township roads and still find nothing but fields, more fields, and the same road running ahead.

I often see the edge of town, the sky and its towering and shifting formations of clouds, that beautifully lit emptiness, when I am writing. But I've never been able to describe it as well as the Danish writer Isak Dinesen, even though she was writing not of the American Great Plains but about the high plains of Kenya.

"Looking back," she says, in her reminiscence *Out of Africa*, "you are struck by your feeling of having lived for a time up in the air. The sky was rarely more than pale blue or violet, with a profusion of mighty, weightless, everchanging clouds sailing on it, but it had a blue vigour in it, and at a short distance it painted the ranges of hills and woods a deep fresh blue. In the middle of the day the air was alive over the land, like a flame burning; it scintillated, waved, and shone like running water, mirrored and doubled all objects. Up in this high air you breathed easily, drawing in a vital assurance and lightness of heart. In the highlands you woke up in the morning and thought: Here I am, where I ought to be."

Here I am, where I ought to be.

A writer must have a place where he or she feels this, a place to love and be irritated with. One must experience the local blights, hear the proverbs, endure the radio commercials, go to reservation churches, roundhouses, cafés, and bingo palaces. By the close study of a place, its people and character, its crops, products, paranoias, dialects, and failures, we come closer to our reality. It is difficult to impose a story and a plot on a place. However, truly knowing a place forms the suggestive basis for every kind of linking circumstance. Location, whether it is to abandon it or draw it sharply, is where we start.

In our own beginnings, we are formed out of the body's interior landscape. For a short while, our mothers' bodies are the boundaries and personal geography which are all that we know of the world. Once we emerge we have no natural limit, no assurance, no grandmotherly guidance like the Tewa, for technology allows us to reach beyond the layers of air that blanket earth. We can escape gravity itself, and every semblance of geography, by moving into sheer space. And yet we cannot escape our need for reference, identity, or our pull to landscapes that mirror our most intense feelings.

The Macondo of Gabriel García Márquez, Faulkner's Yoknapatawpha County, and the island house of Jean Rhys in *The Wide Sargasso Sea* are as real to me as any place I've actually been. And although fiction alone may lack the power to head our government leaders off the course of destruction, it affects us as individuals and can spur us to treat the earth, in which we abide and which harbors us, as we would treat our own mothers and fathers. For once we no longer live in the land of our mother's body, it is the earth with which we form the same dependent relationship, relying completely on its cycles and elements, helpless without its protective embrace.

The Way the Country Lies

From the back porch of my parents' farmhouse, the house I left for college more than twenty years ago, you can look out past a brief yard bordered by a wooden fence which my father's fastidious maintenance keeps a white as fresh as hope, past a small vegetable garden just beyond the fence and then to the fields running south to a two-lane highway. And beyond the highway to the fields of another farm. And beyond those fields to a faint clean seam where they run into the sky at the edge of the earth.

In the first week of February the Iowa winter is performing mythically. The air is clear and relatively windless and the sun strikes with an intensity that applies a luster to the snow. From the heated comfort of the thermal-paned porch where my father and I sit, the beauty of the day asks you to join it, and if you were to accept the invitation you would find its temperature to be twelve below zero.

My father shifts in his wicker chair. He is a short, slight man in his late sixties, with a full head of silver hair that begins in a prominent wave. He habitually points with his right hand when he speaks, a gesture that has held a deep fascination for me since he lost its index finger in a metal press some years ago. Surgically re-styled, his hand has a sculptural slenderness that newly interests me every time I see him, and I often catch myself admiring its lovely knuckled elegance.

Pointing broadcast to the winter day from which we're sealed, he says, "Old Jack Beechum. Boy, now there's a guy, he's in *terrible* shape."

I'm confused, hearing the phrase to mean that someone's very ill ("Mabel's in terrible shape. Her color's awful."), which is what it used to mean when spoken here. "How so?" I ask.

"Well, he sold his farm to his son. But the son's gone bankrupt and let the farm go back. Now Jack's got it on his hands again when he thought he was out from under it. And if the son's bankrupt you figure he hasn't made any payments on it."

Which is what the phrase means when spoken here today. Iowa is in terrible shape. Its color, its true color, economically, psychologically, not the milky glaze of its February fields, is awful. I've known this, of course, as the rest of the country has known it, through newspaper stories and evening news reports. And I've known it more specifically from my parents' letters and conversations during their visits with me in Boston. But in the first years of the trouble, 1981, 1982, the central part of Iowa, where our home place near Prairie City sits, continued relatively unharmed, somewhat insulated from an immediate vulnerability by the simple excellence of its soil and by rain which the more meager hummocky land in the southern part of the state did not receive.

As he talks, my father looks out, his gaze fixed. He tells me of a high-school classmate of mine who has lost his hardware store, a business he assumed from his father-in-law. And of another classmate's liquidation sale of his farm north of town. Farmers often speak to someone at their side while holding their eye on the horizon, as though, pleased as they may be to pass the time with you, no mere human can draw their full attention from the preoccupant event of the earth against the air. It was one of the earliest proofs that I have no temperament for farming that the spectacle of the view does not yield itself to me. What do farmers see? I've asked myself. Sometimes I've kidded my father that he believes he must keep a sentry's watch or else the scene will anarchically scramble—

the horizon line will leap and ripple, the sky sneak closer. And sometimes I've wondered if my father, other farmers, are still trying to convince themselves, arguing with the deductions of Columbus, for a life of field work, tractors moving back and forth, field edge to field edge over the most minimally gradient land, must regularly reinforce the sense that the earth is unarguably flat.

He says, "And they say C——'s bouncing checks high as a ball. P—— says he paid him for some work he did the other day with a check countersigned by the FHA. Nobody knows how C——'s holding on." He mentions in a single reflection five or six people I know, my age or somewhat older, whose farming lives are finished or, in the collective wisdom of the town's feverish gossip, certainly imperiled. Pausing, he gently places his hand in his lap with an apparent consciousness, as though it were a pet. The mannerism arises not from any sense of handicap but from heredity. I remember his father sitting on this porch after coming in from these fields to wait to be called for the huge noon meal, arranging his own massive hands in the same lovingly considered way.

So much has changed since the last time we sat on this porch to talk purely about the fiscal side of farming. Then, nearly ten years ago, he was considering whether to buy from his sister her half of the farm their father had purchased in 1936, or to join her wish to sell and offer all 147 acres as a piece. I remember asking him then if he'd thought what might have happened if I'd been good at farming and had wished to farm with him, and he'd spoken of the problems such an interest would have caused. How he'd have been forced to seek more land to sustain a partnership, as many farmers in the area were doing for their sons. And then, meeting my thoughts directly, he said, "No, I never minded that you weren't interested. Because, in fact, I never loved farming myself."

That moment will remain imperishable for its casual absolution and for his quiet admission. Because I'd long ago made in my mind a naive equation: he was so good at farming, obeisant to his fields; therefore, he must certainly be motivated by an ardor matching his gifts. But no. What had moved him, he went on to say, had been his father's pressing wish that he take over the farm, and after complying he practiced a life for forty years which he was dispassionately very good at.

And now, as I see the conditions of farms and read that those farmers hardest hit are exactly those my age who began to farm when I would have begun, I realize my father's greatest gift to me: he didn't love the work.

I look out at the fields and see an early lifetime of my mistakes, some of them hilarious in their recollection from the safe distance of twenty years. Tractors backed up over rotary hoes. Disks mangled in fences. The stuff of movie stunts. For me, as a teenager driving a tractor with the season's applicable implement attached, farming remained always, and inappropriately, an act of play. I loved the manual intimacies of the work too closely—the flow of the tractor's power from the steering wheel, through my hands and up into my shoulders; the mixture of field dust and the sun's unbroken glare and my free sweat, defining a labor of incredible sensuality. Consequently, the literal efforts of farming began and ended right there for me, at the wheel, as a simplistically pleasurable chore. I was never quite able to sense, or accept, that what I was doing had consequences outside the moment of myself atop a tractor, churning dust, taking heat. That is a lack, a blindness to the dimensions of farming, as incurable as an absence of speed and coordination in an aspiring athlete. I could not look back over my shoulder at the raking pattern of a harrow I was pulling and gauge whether or not it was breaking the earth at the proper depth and angle. I could not see the patterns in the soil as a farmer can, and must. And I could never quite believe that it mattered that I should.

Also, because the act of farming was recreation, I couldn't stay continuously attentive to the business I was conducting and often went far into fantasies, a luxurious inattention a farmer cannot allow himself. I invented World Championship Disking competitions, in which I, speeding elegantly across the field atop our lumbering rust-red Case tractor, steered to another first-place finish. Or, later, in my teens, I simply dreamed, or sang to myself, making up country-western lyrics describing unspeakable love-grief, then came back in my mind to the fields passing beneath me to see that I'd strayed for half a mile far to the left of where I needed to be.

This is what I see when I look out at the fields, and because my work with my grandfather and my father was understood early on by all of us to be whatever help I could give them and no sort of serious apprenticeship, the calamities I summon in my memory make me smile.

Ten years ago, when my father and I talked, there was a swatch of weedy barnyard beyond the white fence. There was a long aluminum shed out there housing my father's outdated machinery. This porch on which we're sitting was half its present size and uninsulatedly porous, and the house it extends from had not been shored up and thoroughly resurfaced in and out.

These fields, surrounding the house on three sides, were openly coveted ten years ago. Men came to the porch door, or came as intermediaries for those only slightly acquainted with my father, to ask if he would sell them. Considering what to do, thinking it might be time, knowing his sister's wish, he watched the prices of farms grow—$1,500 an acre, $1,750, $2,340—like a freakishly nutrient crop, and when he finally set his figure, $3,400 an acre, the man he offered it to spent less than a day deciding it was a price he should take before it rose.

"I was a little surprised," he says, "he decided so quick. But I told him at the time I honestly didn't think it was too high a price, compared. And he'd bought a lot of the land around us, so I figured he wanted it purty bad." He adds, "I didn't have to sharpen a pencil to figure, at that price, it didn't pay me to own it."

Those like myself for whom this view has no distracting hold don't see that the landscape, apparently so still, must be as animate as the roll of the ocean. This comes to me as I realize that in fact everything about the view from our porch has changed. Ten years ago, these fields were expensive and unsubtly desired. They were also, then, my father's. Now, by all appearances unchanged, the view is not at all the same one. It's owned and farmed by someone else and it's worth roughly nine hundred dollars an acre. Maybe that has much to do with what keeps the farmer's eye fascinated. He sees the very definitions of the land continuously changing, or at most briefly poised; he sees, in both senses, the way the country lies.

I look at my father and cannot imagine the struggle he'd be having right now if he'd not sold when he did. Thank God, I think. His farming has been honed to the care of a vegetable garden and the obsessive mowing of a two-acre lawn, the land around the house my parents have kept, and the maintenance of the bordering white fence whose job, one might reasonably conclude, is to keep another farmer's fields from coming any closer.

Conditions have reached so completely into the quotidian that one begins to see the constant reminders of them composing a kind of funereal undersong which the people no longer quite consciously hear. I pick up a recent day's *Des Moines Register* from a stack in the living room my mother has been saving for me and read, on its front page, that Iowans are flocking to pawnbrokers in Des Moines to get what cash they can to meet the Christmas season's bills. And, on the same page, that a banker in the small town of Lenox was shot at through the window of his home, presumably by someone angered at his reluctance to extend farmers' loans. And, still on the front page, that a small boy has received an anonymous one-thousand-dollar check from someone who'd seen a television report on the emotional suffering of farmers' children. The boy's mother has a life-threatening kidney disease and his diabetic father, with no money for insulin, has recently lost a farm that had been in his family for more than a century.

A highway billboard just beyond the town limits posts an advertisement for the local farmers' cooperative, assuring those reading it that "together we will put *profit* back into farming."

The radio news announces that the Farmers Home Administration will begin sending letters of notice to farmers three years delinquent in their loans and that anyone receiving one should respond as instructed if he wishes to retain the right of appeal.

Of course all this is, deliberately, no more than the reporting and reflection of current Iowa news, but its collusive effect is to keep in place a low despair, a subliminal propaganda no less effective for being unintentional.

I sit at the kitchen table on a Monday night, reading the stories with a visitor's avidity and talking to my mother as she prepares supper. She stands at the kitchen counter, a short and still handsome woman dressed in beige slacks and a loose striped blouse. Her gray hair surrounds her face in a globe of tight waves. She chops carrots and radishes with a precision that makes a food processor's work appear uneven. In a corner of the room, a radio plays, pausing at the hour to give the news—the lock of deep cold that's still on the state, the University of Iowa's basketball loss to Minnesota, and, midway through the list of stories, the early-evening discovery of a farmer in Melbourne, some forty miles from Prairie City, who'd killed himself that afternoon, a shotgun to his head, "apparently distraught over the farm crisis."

My attention jumps from the paper. "Jesus," I say to my mother, "did you hear that?"

She looks up from her work. "Hear what?" she asks.

Pete Brent swivels in his desk chair and shakes his head. "I suppose you heard we lost another one last night," he says.

I say yes, I'd heard about it on the radio and I ask him if he knows of anyone taking his life who has talked to him on his Hot Line.

"So far, no," he says, tapping his knuckles on the top of his desk. "Oh, I've kept a few of 'em talking while somebody else here called the sheriff or the guy's minister and sent them out to him. I had a guy call and say he was gonna do himself in. He had a shotgun. We got somebody to him in time. He'd tried once before, I guess. Slit his wrists. When they're tellin' ya the details, you know they're serious about it."

Brent works for an activist group called Prairie Fire, one of the number that together make up the Iowa Farm Unity Coalition, perhaps the state's most liberal farmers' organization, having grown from the early recognition in 1981 that people were being put off their land. It seems indicative of the way Pete Brent thinks that he gathers beneath the cover of the pronoun *we* the man from Melbourne who shot himself Monday night: *We lost another one. . . .* He was an Iowan. He farmed. He was, therefore, one of us.

He moves constantly in his desk chair as he talks, leaning forward with his elbows on his knees, then swinging in his chair to look out his window at the second-story view of downtown Des Moines, its office buildings sprouting, like a weather-riddled crop, in clusters widely separated by sky.

He squirms for a comfortable position, seems a boy sentenced to his desk at recess while his classmates play outdoors. And in a way he is. For most of his working life he was a farmer, at play outdoors, most recently raising cattle on a farm just west of Des Moines, and in every way he remains one except that he no longer has cattle or a farm on which to raise them. Brent declared his operation bankrupt last year and his work for Prairie Fire has grown from volunteering to answer the phones to the full-time position he holds now, supervising its Farm Crisis Hot Line, taking many of its calls. Twenty to twenty-five a day, lasting fifteen minutes to an hour and a half.

He wears blue jeans, ankle-high boots, a flannel shirt, a goose-down vest. He has thin blond hair and a healthy flush that a man with a desk job has no right to have, and I decide that Brent continues on his land so completely in spirit that his attitude puts the hue of a farmer in his face.

He says, of the people who call this office now, "They're more and more depressed. There's more helplessness in them. We're at the point now, we're losing guys've been struggling for three and four years. I tell them, 'Hey, stick it out. It's like readin' a book. Don't you want to know how it's gonna end?'"

Brent says of his methods with those who call, "I tell them they got to start sharing information and their feelings with me. They got to open up if I'm gonna help them. If you keep them talking you got a chance." He says, "I had a guy the other day. He calls up, says, 'Is this the suicide hot line?' I told him, 'We been called a lot of things but that's a first. Now what's goin' on? What're they doin' to you?'"

More than anything I've learned, the idea of farmers in such conversations on the phone, advising one another to speak their feelings—twenty, thirty calls a day, one farmer admitting to another he's been hearing about those who've killed themselves and he's thinking it just might be the best idea left—more than anything yet, this seems to me the measure of the culture's desperation.

Not the suicides themselves. In a way, a farmer killing himself is the sadly logical extreme of the representative temperament, one of such thorough reserve that any emotion—even, in better times, the high ones—enfolds upon itself for the sake of a public evenness. Knowing the degree to which these people are likely to hold to their manner, it's not hard to understand a despondency made so large, in part by refusing it its voice, that one decides at last to ease it; and after that, decides the way to ease it is to kill it.

What's astonishing to me are those farmers who call Pete Brent instead. I'm not sure, frankly, how excessive it is to claim that, for a farmer so severely pressured, his more difficult option is making a phone call to say that he's in misery. I'm not sure. But I believe with some certainty that it's the less instinctive one. So the insistent ringing of Prairie Fire's hot line and the appearance of many other groups throughout the state whose offers of counsel are drawing strong response give evidence of a midwestern rural psyche shaken deeply enough to show some signs of change, to be forced by fear to open.

We speak for a time, or Pete Brent does, and at the end he thinks once more of himself on the farm and tells me some things that make me consider again what the farmer sees when he investigates his view.

"I hadn't made any money for three or four years when I went under," he says. "But that was all right. It's just Mother and I now, all the kids are gone, and her job could take care of the two of us. And geez, I was willing to sit out there and work for free if they'da just let me stay on. See," he says, his voice both high and full, "the problem with farmers, where all this anguish is comin' from, when they take away his farm they take everything. I mean, they take his heart and his soul, but they also take his dream."

As Pete Brent's volume grows I glance left through the door to the outer office, where three men work mutedly at desks in a row and answer the constantly ringing telephones. They are dressed as Brent is, like farmers, and, as he was one, so were they. Sitting near the doorway, party to the marvelously exhortative air in one room, witness to the laconic efficiency in the other, I understand what I'd felt when I entered the offices an hour ago and one of the men looked up at me, raising his eyes as minimally as possible, and nodded a wordless greeting, making it my turn then to speak. It was as though I'd walked into a feed store or the co-op, any place where farmers routinely gather to trade their conversant silence. That's precisely what Prairie Fire's offices feel like, a shop on the square where farmers pause before heading out to their places to resume the work. But these men are not pausing before returning to work; the work they have is here.

Brent continues, his voice crackling upward to an adolescent register. "A farmer, he works in his fields and he's thinkin', 'Next year I'll take out those trees,' or 'I'll put more fertilizer on that piece,' or 'I'll put up fence over there.' Always thinking, projecting into the future, see? It's his dream, he's totally immersed in it. He's never wanted to do any other thing but farm and all he's got in mind now is either he'll die on the place or his kids'll take it over.

"And now he gets his dream taken away from him, and when you don't have your dream no more . . . Geez, I mean, take my heart if you gotta, take my soul, but don't take away my dream."

He says nothing more and the room is abruptly quiet. Even the phones seem to hold for several moments.

After I've said good-bye to Pete Brent and the office's outer door closes, I stand in the hallway to put on my stocking cap and gloves for the bright frozen day. And then I hear from inside a loose round of laughter and someone says, "I have to say, Pete. It just by God makes my day to come in here and listen to you talk!" And someone else says, "Man, Pete. I thought I's gonna have to come in there and throw water on you. I never heard you lay it on so thick before." And more laughter, and I think I hear Brent's amused, squeaking protest.

I smile. Yes. Exactly as men in the feed store would laugh among themselves after the stranger had been ushered out the door. But it's not that Brent was merely performing for a visitor's willing innocence. It's that still, and even here in the offices of a Farm Crisis Hot Line that people call to say they're thinking of killing themselves, even here the rooms must be quickly swept after the open display of such emotion, words like *heart* and *soul* and *dream* moving boisterously in the air.

Driving the highway from Des Moines, through Prairie City and on out toward my parents' house east of town, I have Pete Brent's words still in my head.

The highway leaves Prairie City, bends easily left, straightens for a mile or so, then curves sharply right at Warrick's Corner, named for the family whose farm occupies the curve, an infamously dangerous turn that has taken several local lives in car accidents over the years.

There are five farms between the edge of town and the intersecting road to my parents' place, and I know who lives in each of them, have an overlapping impression, a kind of *pentimento* of memory and present, of each place as I pass it now and simultaneously pass it all the times I have before. But if I sense a fusion of history and moment, the farms themselves have physically produced that fusion.

Through the left-hand sweep, the road rising with the land. On my left, a recently built one-story house, plain as a coffin, beside the larger original place. The man who lived with his family in the former lives by himself in the new one, not fifty yards away. And across the road, the same pattern—a small new house, spare as the dimensions of a pared-down life, a hundred yards west of the old one, standing shabbily in decline. Past Warrick's Corner, to the farm at the crossroads. And here also, a tiny frame house sprung up against the highway, surrounded in winter by unimpeded winter air. And behind it, the oddly slender structure which the owners, an unmarried brother and sister, used to live in. Someone says that cats live in it now. My father says that when the two of them moved across the yard they painted the old place for the first time in years. Why in heaven's name, he wonders, would they wait to paint it now. Maybe, I suggest, because now it is their view.

I've often thought about the tight line of life traced by those who are raised and stay and die here. The way one can stand at the beginning of life and sight uninterruptedly down it, to its end in the Clearview Manor nursing home at the northern edge of the town across the road from the cemetery. These were the steps of my Grandmother Bauer's life, for one. The burden of that clarity has always been incomprehensible to me, one of the reasons this way of life has never seemed spacious and easy to move about in, but just the opposite—densely cluttered with the reduplicating presence of one's past and with the awful claustrophobia of knowing your particularly specific end. No one likes to feel crowded, I've replied to local people who ask me how I can possibly live in cities; that's why I can't live here.

But after hearing the testimony of Pete Brent, I think of the security farming people feel in a life on one piece of earth, the pull of the pleasures of its absolute routine. I have always thought of farming as a way of life filled with nothing but recurrent risk, and I think it's fair to say that that's the prevalent view. The risk of weather, of prices, of all manner of things beyond the farmer's control. Perhaps I felt this so conclusively for remembering my father's palpable anxiety as a farmer, worrying his crop home every year, standing on the porch, the old, porous porch, at the end of the day and pragmatically searching the sunset's splendor for the weather he needed in the morning.

Now, as I drive toward the house, it occurs to me that what the farmer has always felt for the life so many are losing is not its risk at all, but its absence of risk, its firm certainty. No matter how severe the hail, how desiccating the drought, the life of farming continued. All the wrenching vicissitudes played out within the inviolate law of people's need to eat. Even in the first depression, when farms also failed epidemically, the way of life remained or was eventually reclaimed after years of disruption. It's been striking to me how many men have begun to talk about these times by saying, "My dad lost his farm in the Depression." Every one who's said this is a farmer, or has been one until forced from his farm. And the frightening prospect now is that there will be no such thing as farming to return to.

How extraordinary. To think that the lure of the life has always been its reliability. I imagine a farmer, year after year, growing old with the ceremony, opening the earth and placing his seeds, the *sureness* of the life, until he achieves a perfectly reductive sublimity and dies on the land in the way he has lived, solemnly placed, his last seed, in his soil.

It's this certainty that farmers need, to be able to predict their clean and ordered steps toward death. Pete Brent believes they value it so deeply they consider it their dream, thinks they'd work for nothing to keep it out there in their sights: *to die on the place or leave it to their kids.*

He may be right. I can't think of a better definition of a dream. Not as I pass the farms that flank the highway and envision, inside any one of them, the farmer standing at the window of his original house, at first light in early May, his newly turned fields gleaming blackly, and allowing himself the luxury of his full imagination. Where, he asks himself, is the perfect place to end? Where would I build a last house? And then smiles to himself as its image slowly forms, at the end of his life at the end of his field.

I turn left toward my parents' house. Ahead, it stands massively, the landscape around it as clean as that of a just completed suburb's. With some of the money from the sale of the farm they radically altered the house's shape but kept its scale. They built a bedroom on the first floor so that, eventually, neither of them will have to climb the stairs. They rearranged the layout so that they could enter the basement without having to go outside. It seems to me so changed that I always have a few minutes of real disorientation whenever I visit, unthinkingly anticipating the house that it had been.

Early March is never done well in Iowa. The snow has melted and there's a subtly variegated gray on all its surfaces, the sky, the land, the faces of the buildings. So it's impossible to know whether the town of Prairie City has deteriorated further since last summer, when I'd last visited and noticed signs of decline, or if what appears a deeper bleakness, a kind of sourceless soot, is only the value of the light.

Still, there are some things I see and know for sure. A magnificent old house, a block from the square, preposterously gabled, always my favorite house in town, is sliding into ruin. The buildings of the lumberyard that dominate the west edge of the town badly need the paint they've always gotten almost prematurely. Uptown, the Please-U Cafe in the middle of the block on the north side of the square has recently reopened. For forty years or more, the Please-U had been the place where everyone came at some point during the day, a sort of conversational roundhouse. But its owner, Snub DeWit, retired and sold it four years ago, and the woman who bought it quickly ran out of money and it closed. Now, still another owner is trying to bring it back.

Without the Please-U, the town's social currency, its gossip, has settled more diffusely—in the bank's waiting area, in the aisles of the convenience market, and in the two small drive-ins on the through-town highway that took the Please-U's business and its talk. But in fact there now seems so much talk, and so much need to, that I cannot imagine the Please-U alone would have been able to hold it. I suspect it still would have spilled out the front door and pooled agitatedly in all the places that it has.

"I heard P—— was drunk as a bat in his pickup Saturday morning. L—— came into the car wash and there he was sprawled out on his front seat."

"You know why, don't ya?"

"Bankruptcy?"

"That's what I get."

"R—— called in his order for a fuel delivery this morning."

"So?"

"It's the first time in all the years I've worked here he didn't just say, 'Fill the tanks.' He said exactly how many dollars to deliver and it didn't come near fillin' his tanks."

"Is that right? So R——'s feeling it. Wonder how much longer he's got."

If the talk has found more places, its subject has narrowed to a singular obsession. How's *he* doing? How's *he* keep from goin' under? Everyone in Prairie City has been reduced to the biographical essence of his life in relation to the enveloping threat. There goes B——. He let his farm go back this fall. Lookit T—— and R——. How're they living, now that he's bankrupt? There's D——. Lookit that lucky sumbitch. Sold out jist in time and livin' off the interest.

My father, of course, is a lucky sumbitch in the eyes of the town, his most accomplished act of farming the orchestration of his quitting it. He says he's sometimes teased about his good fortune, as he sits with his friends in a booth at the drive-in, but that others here were also able to sell profitably a few years ago, leaving him a few people to talk to. In fact, what he's more often asked is whether or not the man who bought the farm has been keeping up his payments. He's asked that question almost weekly, he says. He's been asked if the check he receives has begun to be co-signed, as the rumor tells it these days. It has not, my father has patiently replied.

Today, March 1, is the date when farmers historically have moved onto the new places they've bought or rented. My grandfather moved from his old farm north of Colfax to his new one east of Prairie City on March 1, 1936, exactly fifty years ago today. It is also the date when farmers traditionally make payments on their farms and so, predictably I suppose, my father was asked this morning if the man who'd bought his farm had been keeping up his payments. Yet it saddens me to think that a man's farming history, anyone's here, not just my father's, has been simplistically condensed by the monotonous curiosity about all that matters now.

My parents and I sit at supper the night before I leave. It is, beneath all the change in their lives and in the feel of this house, the rhythm I can instinctively find. We sit at the places at the table where we sat when I was growing up; only the chair of my brother, who's a generation younger than I and equally uninterested in farming, sits empty between my mother and father.

We trade easy conversation, a family reporting on its day. Behind my mother, the kitchen door is open to let the heat of her cooking out and to let the weather in. It has become in a day as warm as the soft heat of June. We argue genially about whether the train still stops in Colfax, try to reconstruct the line of succession of the Methodist Church ministers from my high-school days until now.

I've come to realize that what I'll lose if Prairie City dies is my most uncompromising mirror. I've looked more closely at the town in the past week than I have for ten years, and what I've seen, beyond the predominant decline that's obvious to everyone and seems nearly immediate to me, is a subtler flow of change. The myth of small places includes their timelessness, but only those who stay in them are privileged to live with that perception. For those who have left and periodically return, the sense of change—more exactly, of age—is dramatic. In the faces of people you last saw three years ago, and two years before that, but saw, just as memorably, when you were six, and ten, and seventeen. Or in now-shadeless streets, after Dutch elm disease, that had received huge blankets of shadow from the trees that used to line them. Or in noticing that there's now a wire mesh fence at the edge of an outfield that had been infinitely borderless when you played it. Seeing unmistakably how Prairie City ages, I've always seen, therefore, that I must have aged as well.

So I want the town and the life here to change and age with a natural procedure. That way, when I return, and must look squarely into it, I can see myself, congruent with its easy, measured advance. But instead, it's being brutally hurried to an end or to something so fundamentally destructive that it's the same thing. If it dies, I'll have nothing more accurately reflecting than the dubious specter of memory, literally no way of life to have left.

Yet that seems to me as I think about it an incredibly precious complaint. I do, after all, have a way of life I'll resume tomorrow, after a plane flight, and the people who farm Iowa very soon may not.

But there's something more legitimately integral touched by the threat of this life's passing. I came some years ago to recognize the ways in which I was formed by the habits of the culture, the parts of me that are, if not a farmer, some strong reflection of the abiding cadences. I see my inordinate regard for an orderly life, a kind of grid of work and clearly scheduled leisure, a routine calibrated like the topography of Iowa with its squarely sectioned fields and the strict symmetry of its lanes and roads. I spent a long time wishing I weren't so needful of this order; it made me seem to myself some humorless actuary, until I understood where it came from and, after that, I gradually settled into an amused accommodation with instincts I could see as the Iowan in me.

I've come to realize, as well, how closely my work is a form of my father's. Farming and writing share features of isolation, independence, the planting of a crop with no assurance of a harvest. I think I've become comfortable with the patience writing requires because I learned when I was twelve that when I started down a row I would be following it for miles before there was a release from its requirements. And that, reaching row's end, I would swing around and start back down again. Work, like my own, of severe recurrence. Except that I have found a way to farm without needing to attend to the restrictions of the soil. I can sight the length of a field to an end I can't see and head off toward it, singing loudly to myself, inventing lyrics not merely tolerated by the work but requisite for it. I've learned that a writer is the farmer of meandering rows. And the farmer in me resents the threat to farming deeply.

"The hardest thing to decide," my mother says, clearing dishes, "was not to buy your aunt's piece of the farm. Because once we decided that, it meant we had to sell. We knew we couldn't get along on just the piece we'd be left with."

In his chair at my left, my father nods, seeming to be thinking about those conversations.

"I realized today," I say, "I haven't actually walked out into the fields since you sold the farm. I feel like a trespasser or something, I guess." I look at my father. "Do you feel like that at all?"

He says he doesn't, and speaks of a corner of his acreage that's never been fenced, so that the fields touch his neatly mown lawns. "I asked him if I could stack some branches we cleared along there and he said, sure, no problem. So with him, it's never been a big deal."

But that doesn't answer what I'm asking, and I say more plainly,

"Yeah, but what do you think when you see him farming the land?"

"Well," my father says, "actually, it's been gratifying to see how he's improved it. He's laid a whole lot of tile so it drains a lot better." He reminds me of low places that some years stayed too muddy to work after a long rain. "And he's put down a lot of lime. These fields needed liming something awful to cut the acid in the soil."

Selfishly, I'm still after something else, some expression of complex ambivalence I'm projecting onto him. "But doesn't it make you feel weird sometimes, to watch him out there?"

Generously, my father smiles. "Oh, sure," he says softly. "You'd have to be weird *not* to feel weird sometimes."

"And," I continue, "I was wondering today, walking around town, do you ever feel, I don't know, some kind of guilt that you made out so well with all this going on now?"

He looks at me with the closest thing to irritation that ever comes into his eyes. Not so much with me, I think, as with the absurdity of the notion. "Lord, no," he answers. "You'd have to be dumb to think something like that." And once again he's cut through the impractical aimlessness he sees in some concern of mine and has given it back to me with a simplicity that, in its firmness, I've sometimes likened to the awarding of grace.

We push our chairs back and carry plates to the sink and fall into our assignments. My mother washes. I dry. My father scrapes the most resistant pans, sacks the garbage.

The window above the sink gives to simple depthless night but, nevertheless, after ten days here, I have the fields behind the darkness on my mind. It's still amazing to me to think that farmland has begun to be thought of as a kind of curse. I remember the frenzied need to acquire more and more of it and hear now about people who thought they were "free" of it and then, through others' failures, have had to take it back. I hear people urging others to stop being so proud, to admit their debt and "let the farm go back," that curious phrase, as though if released a piece of land would, on some primal impulse, rush back to where it came from. *Let the land go. Good God, get rid of it.*

My father tells me that he has no concern in that regard. "The way I sold it, I got enough of a down payment so that even if I did have to take it back, I could sell it again even at these prices and make out all right."

But of course he'd not wish to do that; it would alter the earned perfection of his view, which I think I've begun in a way to understand. At this point in his life, he can sit inside the prosperous ease of his large last house and look out at the measureless sweep of all that he has done. It's neither a place nor a view that I would—that I could—choose, since I know I couldn't live with the congestion of the fields.

DAVID HAMILTON

American Gothic

"No tridents around here.
Who carries a pitchfork?"
—Henry W. Hamilton

GEOGRAPHY

Ideally called Fairville, Bloomfield, Fairfield, Belle
Plaine, Pleasant Plain, What Cheer, or Blue Earth,
midwestern small towns, clustering under a wide
sky, reduce in the mind's eye to single, complex structures. Traceries of streets, and even more of contact and consciousness, run
among the people and their places. Like a squirrel making a course
of the trees in some backyards, your eye may veer off in any number of directions but need never be checked by a gap.

My hometown, like many others, spreads from the intersection
of two U.S. highways. A much smaller river town fourteen miles
north had once seemed more promising, but railroads reversed all
that, leaving our town, toward the center of the county, the land-locked focus. The square marked its center, and the highways approximately quartered the whole. Each quadrant had its grade
school—Northwest, Southeast, Benton, and Eastwood—deflections from consistency, being, I suppose, a virtue.

Three of the four grade schools economized on the same architectural design: a U of hallway, with classrooms arranged along its
outer side, embracing a small auditorium and gym. Our high
school was essentially two grade schools stacked. Its U was longer

and broader, with more classrooms opening off it, and the auditorium contained a balcony, a stage, and a full-sized basketball
court; but its shape was the same. Northwest, the eccentric, two-
storied grade school, had been the town's original school.

THE COURTHOUSE

Our town had a courthouse and a square. The courthouse featured a soaring dome over a square tower with clocks, and
light bulbs outlined the dome's four, soft, curving ridges. Except
during the energy crisis of the seventies, that courthouse has been
a landmark from afar. Even now when approaching the town after
a long absence, I strain before I'm quite conscious of it and watch
for my first glimpse of the dome rising above the trees. As a boy,
riding into town with my parents, usually standing behind the
front seats with my brother, and especially after dark, we would
vie to see it first, to catch its luminescence against the sky. Had I
read Fitzgerald by then, I might have thought of the glittering
yellow outline as a tent hovering above our oaks and elms and her-
alding a party. Now, two sets of grain elevators rise into the same
skyline, muddying that old invitation.

For someone like me, returning to town means dipping beneath
the courthouse to the memory of our schools. They dominated
my consciousness during the years I lived there. For from one
point of view, the town is a series of age-groups stacked up more
or less like the floors of the high school. For those who stay, ver-
tical as well as horizontal connections come to bind the whole together, in knowledge and acquaintance, if not in community and
sympathy throughout. But for those who leave after high school,
the horizontal tracery of one's age-group goes farthest toward
comprehending the town we knew.

"My uncle would have called it an 'eminence,'" I say to myself while my car, taking me home, curves over a knoll and dips toward a creek with its cottonwoods and straggling soft maples. A couple of oaks stand out in the foreground and a hog lot opens around them, a few weathered farrowing sheds, feeders with their flapping tin lids, and a sprinkling of beasts coming into sluggishness for our tables. Any rise in the land as high as their haunches might have been an "eminence."

One I remember well was the seat of a new tractor. It was winter; my father and uncle had been clearing land, and the shiny, red Massey-Harris in our basement awaited its first use the next spring. That winter, I spent hour after hour in the tractor seat, my hand on the wheel, my self in charge, my eyes making a vista of the basement wall, seeing past the lumber and tools stacked, a log chain and sections of hose, toward acres and acres of wheat, wheat as far as I could imagine, and a roll in the landscape, the space of Canada or Kansas. The Korean War had begun and my mission was to keep our troops provided.

Another eminence lay behind our house on Eastwood, which had no companion streets to the north or south, only pastures and woods, a remnant of the country. Leaving my house by the back door, running past the garage and a chicken coop my younger brother had commandeered as a clubhouse—membership depended on our dropping at least one forbidden word into each sentence we uttered—then through an unused garden with an arbor of Concord grapes, I'd jump a drooping fence, bear right, and within twenty yards or so, the trail rising slightly, veer off into a grove of Osage orange on a knoll, one of my several hideouts. Hedge apples they were also called, or bowwood, for Indians favored Osage orange for making bows. A friend of my father's had made us each longbows of Osage orange. I still have my father's and still savor its elegance, though modern archers look askance at technology so primitive.

That grove gave me preliminary command of my territory. Ahead and to my right, the trail dipped down into forest. Almost within sight was a glen—I favored that word from reading *Robin Hood*—where, under what I thought a majestic oak, I experimented setting snares for rabbits. Beyond, the trail became less distinct, though it led to a railroad track and a stream. Beyond that lay the grounds of the State School for the Epileptic and Feeble Minded, a name since changed for reasons of accuracy and humanity both. We called its residents inmates and were always on the lookout for them. Once in a while one would escape and might be found in our woods, more likely wandering drugged and confused than dangerous.

Ahead, also, but to my left lay two unused pastures, with remnants of bluestem and other prairie grasses and our trails running through, along the fencelines and crisscrossing. Sometimes we'd come upon the remains of a fox poisoned by our neighbors, who minded their chicken coop and garden plot and meant to keep them flourishing. Farther west lay more woods. I built a lean-to into one hillside, a rough but fairly permanent retreat. On another, I fashioned a wigwam. From such points of vantage, we could make forays all along the street, on the preacher's house, on Carolie, my cousins, my great aunt and grandmother, on Peggy and her mother, and so on, moving west into town.

FARM

But we were a farm family, almost, the town being half of what I knew. My father and uncle farmed together in the river bottoms north and west of us. Floods were frequent enough to discourage homebuilding out there, so we lived in town and commuted. A rectangle of land, a mile and a half by a half mile, my father and uncle having cleared most of it, the farm was a patchwork of fields, the front field, the new field, the middle field, the house field, the long, narrow field, and the north field. An eminence there was really little higher than a hog's haunch, unless it was the remnant of an old levee, and there was no house in the house field, only a stack of rough-milled boards that had been one. We played on an abandoned combine, left for its value in odd parts.

The north field was heavy with gumbo, and in late summer, usually well cracked; the front field had sandy loam. Half circles of timber, with cottonwoods soaring tallest, stood east in the middle and west in the long, narrow fields. Drainage ditches ran west to east at several places; one of those, bordering the middle field, opened on a marsh with cattails, willows, and redwing blackbirds. A dogwood patch rose out of it onto higher ground, curving back into the middle field. I don't remember any dogwoods, but it was a patch my father and uncle well remembered clearing. Then they left a strip of woods, about the width of a field, between the front and new fields, a reminder to my brother, my two cousins, and me of what the farm had been. Thick with cottonwood, wild plum, mulberry, box elder, and soft maple, it suffered our paths, our hideouts, our approaches to a raccoon's tree or the foxes' den.

EASTWOOD

Back in town, Eastwood was my terrain. Most grade-school mornings, Albert would stop by for me; then we would walk past Carolie's, hoping we might join her, or she us. We'd pick

Johnny up half a mile along the street. He lived next to Sue, who was by that time usually paired with Carolie. Another quarter mile would be Ann's house, and about another quarter the school, at the head of Eastwood Street, which returned to farmlands another mile west. The playground to the side of the school featured a ravine with no improvements, just trees, shrubbery, taller grass. That's the area we favored during recess more than the ball diamond and jungle gym.

All of us happened to live on and so walked the north side of the street. A few doors past Johnny's, Conway joined Eastwood. Tarred rather than paved, it extended about a block, hooked around to the east, and stopped. A cluster of black families lived on it. As I remember, we mostly called them Negroes, politely. But we didn't know their names and hardly recognized faces.

I remember one exception to our official politeness. I had just moved to town and so was seven. I'd come from a town with fewer and less-visible blacks. One afternoon, sitting along Eastwood with new friends, I called Peggy a nigger—probably the first time I said that word aloud and the only time without ironic intent I can remember. Peggy, a grown woman, lived with her mother right on Eastwood, an anomaly within the fabric of our neighborhood. I don't think I called her a nigger to her face, but I said it so she could hear as she passed, experimenting, no doubt. Wielding a coffeepot, she swung around and chased me across the street, all around Harold Mack's house, and deep into his backyard. I was made to apologize, which means she must have spoken to my parents. Only cordial words ever passed between us after that.

I was closer, though, to Reverend Harvey Baker Smith, who also lived only a few doors away. Reverend Smith wore a cutaway when he preached and looked like a retired senator. He had once been chaplain to the United States Congress. I led the youth group of his church for a time, and he meant to make a minister of me.

One summer I got into the habit of coming around to his house to watch the Friday night fights. It was the era of Rocky Marciano, Jersey Joe Walcott, and Ezzard Charles; and it was disturbing, he said, and wrong, to see a black man and a white man fight.

He used that expression, "black man." It sounded strange to me; I sensed its accuracy but was unsure of connotations. I can remember his worried look, as if sparring with matters of state, while he stared hard at the fight and let his ice tea, served by Shelby, his grown daughter, dampen the magazine on the floor beside his couch.

Whatever the year, though, and on most mornings, several black kids would appear from Conway as we were making our way to school. They would cross Eastwood and walk up the south side, in separate procession, as we continued on the north. A block before we came to our school, they turned south again and walked another several blocks to theirs. We never spoke to each other as I recall, hardly eyed each other directly. "Dark cloud moving south," Uncle Henry would say when passing a few blacks on a country road. And so that group appeared to us, moving west then south, while our own small cloud, equally overcast, paralleled them for the block we shared.

As I grew toward independence, I'd walk Eastwood alone, going or coming, at dusk or later. And all through high school I'd feel an edge of unease if I passed a black boy, or man, in the dark, though usually he'd be on the south side and I on the north. If I saw him looming ahead on my own sidewalk, I might cross over myself, affecting an attitude to suggest my real purpose took me there. When I became embarrassed at that poor tactic and chose to hold my ground, I'd steady myself, bring any humming or whistling to a halt, and control my measured pace until we passed. We probably looked at each other, probably nodded. Often I'd break into a run a few steps later, reasoning that I was used to running Eastwood anyway, for practice. If I saw the stranger from far enough away to make it seem I wasn't running just because of him, I'd pass him flying and keep going, holding my stride steady, one step for each of the five-foot sections of the walk, or trying to hold it so till I was out of sight. Meanwhile, my shadow pursued me while it shortened, as I ran under a streetlight, then leapt ahead, lengthening, as I passed it.

CANNING

Summers meant putting up food, canning and freezing. On certain early mornings, my father and uncle and I, and perhaps my brother or cousin, would go to the farm and pick several sacks of sweet corn. We'd have a few rows of it growing along the edge of a field, back just far enough not to be obvious from the road, but planted like the other corn, with the field planter. Or sometimes we'd collect field corn if we caught it on the few days when it was sweet and tender. Then we'd return, usually to my aunt's house. There Mom and Aunt Jean would be making their own preparations, tables and tools set out in the backyard, pots of water near boiling. We'd all set in shucking the corn, then slicing it from the cobs. Okra, beans, peas, asparagus—we put up lots of food—but the corn I remember most. Some we'd can, others package for freezing. Mother would drive us to the locker, and my brother and I would help her carry the packages into the storage room where we'd spend several minutes rearranging things in our rented bins, staying there just long enough, shivering in our T-shirts, to imagine being unable to get out. Then we'd return to the best meal of the year, sweet corn and sliced tomatoes, stacks of the one steaming, slices piled high of the other, and as much as we wanted, my mother's face glowing over each platter she brought to the shared table.

In the winter, my father was usually deep in projects. He worked in our basement, where he had a darkroom and shop. He was a good photographer, and I helped him develop pictures, especially of Indian artifacts. One winter we made a reflecting telescope; we finished grinding a lens he and my mother had begun years before and mounted it so all the neighborhood kids could see the rings of Saturn. Another winter we got some Osage orange blanks from the man who made our bows and worked at making another, shaving and shaving it into shape, until, in our quest for elegance, we went too far, and it cracked. Late one summer, in the season of wild plums, we found a dead coon on a gravel road and my father braked sharply, salvaged the animal, and threw the carcass in the back of the pickup, thinking what I needed most was a genuine coonskin cap. We came right home and set to work in the basement, my father turning old coon over on his back, holding the tail in his left hand, slitting the skin along the belly with the knife in his right. The hide must have been tougher than expected, or the knife duller, for Dad had to dig in, get stiff purchase on the knife, and suddenly the tail snapped right in half. "Shit, piss, fuck, cunt," and I drew back a little, surprised that he, too, knew those words. What a candidate for my brother's club! Even now I can feel their rapid fire and am a little amazed at the unconscious control of assonance and consonance that fixed them in such quick order.

CAROLIE

By the second grade and off and on until college, Carolie, the girl from nearly next door, fueled my dreams. Walking past her house brought me to attention, and I was more than tolerant of her younger brother, about the age of mine, simply because of his access to special knowledge. Her parents owned and ran the drive-in on the northwest side of town, leaving her at home with her grandmother many evenings. They had an extra lot to the side of their house, beside her bedroom window, and an old, cracked swimming pool, never filled, stood in the middle of it. Many a summer evening, I slipped into that pool, watching the soft glow of her window upstairs, the shade always drawn, or at least mostly, but the window like stained glass in my imagination. After a time I'd creep under her window and toss twigs and pebbles against the screen. She'd come and ask, "Who's there," more to be certain than to find out. Then she'd join me on her L-shaped front porch. We'd sit in the swing and talk. We hardly ever touched. Kissing her—clearly the thing to do—was as hard for me as it would have been to cross Eastwood and walk among the blacks, though I was always dreaming of escorting her to one of my places, the lean-to or the wigwam in the woods behind her house. We never had trouble talking; we seemed to know how to say everything except, perhaps, exactly what we felt. Coming close counts for even more in early love than it does in horseshoes.

Then her parents would come home. We'd recognize the car gliding down Eastwood and would still the swing while they turned into the drive and continued back to the garage. As soon as they got behind us, Carolie would slip inside and I off the porch. In my memory, the bridal wreath seems always in bloom. Soon, though, another car was in her drive and another boy on her porch. For by the time serious dating was likely, Carolie's friend-ships ran well beyond our neighborhood, and being pretty, a popular student, and a destined head cheerleader, she awarded the years that mattered to the first-string quarterback in the class ahead of us and the guard with the effortless jump shot in ours.

In the eighth grade, we learned of the Brown decision and that blacks would join us the following year. We still called them Negroes, though not everyone did. Late that spring, an English teacher was protesting that this just wasn't right. The coloreds and the whites weren't the same and shouldn't mix. It would lead to the mongrelization of the species and no good could come from that. She just wouldn't have it, not in her class for sure. God made the two races separate and meant to keep them apart. "Isn't that right?" she asked.

"Maybe God has changed his mind," was Carolie's inspired reply.

The next year, black kids did filter in among us. Some stayed at their own school or had dropped out; they had, as we said, benignly, their choice. Some choice. Their own school, after the eighth grade, was thirty miles south, in another county, by bus. That next year, though, Walter and Eugene came off Conway and joined our classes. They didn't walk to school with us; by then, our ways to high school were more varied anyway. When we were on the street together, though, as long as I can remember, they walked the south side and we the north.

There was at least one exception. Carolie, Eugene, and I were walking home one afternoon, perhaps our junior year. It was clearly an experiment we were improvising together. But overtaking us by car, Carolie's mother squelched it: "Carolie, you get in here right this minute." The invitation was not general. Carolie reminded me of that story at our twenty-fifth reunion, after I'd reminded her of her visionary response in that eighth-grade class. We were telling both our stories to Eugene, who was listening politely and letting us hear him say "black."

I was the eldest of four cousins; fieldwork grew incrementally and gently enough for the three of us who were male. We helped with the later stages of clearing, picking up chunks of wood after the plows had turned the new fields over in the spring, throwing them in piles for burning. We cut off willow sprouts showing in the same season. I had my own axe, smaller than full-size, and axe work has always held some romance for me. I learned to aim beneath the soil, where earth, rewoven through winter, would support those subtle shoots, making your cut firm and clean. But if you struck too high, the sapling would just spring back and the axe quake in your arm and hand.

Eventually we got to tractors. My father was careful not to work us too hard, not a full day when I started at twelve or eleven. Soon my brother could be held back no longer and we shared a tractor, one of us sitting under a cottonwood with a pocket watch making sure the other didn't exceed his hour. From such starts, we grew into full days rapidly enough and, in our better moods, took pride in driving well—backing tractors up so the hitch pin would drop right in the waiting hole of the wagon's beam, tripping and lifting the plow out of the ground and dropping it back in after a tight turn right on line for a new furrow, lifting the cultivator at the end of the field, braking one wheel, turning tightly but smoothly, then dropping the shovels back beside the new rows without taking out a stalk—for one meant four if you got to dreaming.

When it came time to drive, I'd driven tractors and a farm jeep enough to feel at ease behind the wheel. I remember riding to the farm with my father and mother one day as I approached sixteen, and Dad pulled over saying, "I guess Dave had better get some practice." "Can he drive?" Mom inquired. "I expect so," Dad replied, and I slid behind the wheel and drove off. It was easy, though parallel parking took a few tries later that afternoon. The night after I got my license, my parents let me take the jeep out to see friends. One girl told me later how she and her sister and mother had laughed when I came to their house in that funny little car with a motor that sounded like a sewing machine.

TRAFFIC

When we reached driving age, someone always had a car. Whereas my pedestrian knowledge of the town had centered on Eastwood and a few neighboring streets, as far in as the square, cars allowed us to encompass the town in a crisscrossing circuit, and to discover friends who weren't also neighbors. After Sunday School, Saturday afternoons, and most evenings of the week, we would be out and around, and much of the time in a car. We dated, or double-dated, more often cruised with friends. The main circuit was constant. Up Eastwood, around the square, out to Carolie's drive-in on the northwest side; back to the square and south past the high school, to the drive-in on the south edge of town, back in toward the square then straight east to the city park, which was spacious and hilly with its curving drive emptying out on Eastwood about a half mile from my house. Probably by now I have written more paragraphs than I have made circuits of that town, but I can't guess when writing gained the advantage.

For a time during my grade-school years, my father was on the city council, and over dinner he held forth on his objections to widening the square. Widening the streets around it, that is, for the circuit of streets had become the square more than the green within. That meant cutting back the courthouse lawn and cutting down mature oaks and hard maples. It meant installing parking meters, a project only temporarily remunerative. First came a shopping center to the south of town, then another to the west. Now the widened streets look like a school with its windows broken out; the meters have gone and half the parking spaces stand empty.

THE TEENAGE CLUB

Upstairs, over the shops on the northeast corner of the square, between the courthouse and a church, was our teenage club with a snack bar, a room for pool and ping-pong tables, and a dance floor with booths set around it and a jukebox. There was no membership policy that I remember, and no fees. We paid only for candy bars, cokes, and the jukebox. It was open afternoons after school, Saturday and Sunday afternoons, Friday and Saturday nights. Our circuits around town always brought us by the teen-age club, to its shrewd reconciliation of almost all that was inevitable with all still within limits.

We entered through a flapping wooden door off an alley and a parking lot shared with the neighboring church. The door, with no latch, except for a padlock when closed, was the kind you might find on an outhouse. One of the town's two banks faced us right across the street, and the square with the courthouse was catty-corner; we were not on our own exactly. But we could forget to notice. The stairwell, steep, squaring around to the right, gave the sense of an urban tenement, as we could only imagine that from films, or at least of space alone as in an upstairs room or in an attic. Parents never came up there except for the cherubic mother of one schoolmate who managed the place, and familiarity allowed us to ignore her as easily as we shrugged off town management.

The pool and ping-pong rooms opened first off the stairs. Skill at pool, that well-known sign of a misspent youth, was a skill that mattered. If, as my uncle would say, one boy was a boy, two boys were half a boy, and three boys no boy at all, there, a small crowd at pool was distinctly animal, the symbology so flagrant as to be funny. Girls rarely ventured into that room and never hung around there, but they did move back and forth past it. It was a place for adopting a certain swagger, for holding on to your stick, gesticulating firmly, not shaking but pointing, then chalking your tip. Bending over your shot in that peculiarly rigid right angle, you thrust your blue-jeaned butt out as if it were a fist, the bowed crouch of your legs suggesting what they wished to enclose but had turned away from for now. Then the luxurious fondling of the stick, running it back and forth across the notch between your first knuckle and your thumb canted upward, or through the teasing circle made of your left thumb and index finger. Back and forth, back and forth, the cue did its slow dance, back to the lip of the notch and forward, unpartnered but advertising. The rigidity in the posture, the tension in the arms, permitted increasing muscle to flex. Then the controlled violence of the stroke itself, the cue extended and dropped briefly over the felt, the player thrusting himself erect, already in stride for his next shot, the ball rammed home in the pocket. The difference between those who played pool mostly and those who stuck to ping-pong, mostly, was the difference between alpha wolf and the rest.

And it was a whole lot easier to carry off the posture there than in the next room where the girls really were and where there was dancing. In there, the edge came off the swagger. We had our alphas and others of dancing as we did of pool, and they didn't line up exactly. Still, some boys, mostly pool players, were there for business, however much they succeeded. They would be the ones, more often than not, leaving with their girlfriends quickly, hustling them off to cars parked in the alley and to the country roads all around us. Others, who played more ping-pong than pool, might be there more as friends, hanging around as long as time allowed, then going home quietly and unspent.

We spent hours in that room, dancing less than drifting from one booth to another, talking, talking, even playing solitaire, one version known as "Idiot's Delight," a reduce-the-spread-to-one-stack game we could almost play in our sleep, and played usually at a booth with friends. Another feint toward interaction. All this amounted to delay, of course, to be in the place of action without acting greatly. We were mostly "great pretenders" in that era of the Platters, the years just pre-Elvis; and as he came on the scene we were already throbbing. Never more, of course, than when actually dancing, and we all did that too, at varying rates of ability and confidence. Some was fast and separated, barely, the jitterbug leading toward the twist, but the slow stuff counted too—less cheek to cheek than breasts to chest, abdomen to pelvis, the convolutions of arms and sweaters, your right arm, if you were a guy, reaching all the way around her and beginning to brush her right breast, while keeping the irregularities of your erection behind that odd corset of your Levi's zipper.

Of course, the blacks never joined us, and whether they were told not to or whether they never ventured, I cannot say. Integration of the swimming pool was more quickly resolved, democratically and fairly. But the teenage club, with pool and dancing allowed, was still denied, and within a decade more it folded.

SHADY PLACES

The semipermanent tease of the teenage club makes any remaining sense of *off limits* seem banal and silly. Still, every community has its places within easy reach but oddly denied. We had, for example, the Mary Lou Theater, a firetrap, my parents warned, and on the far side of the square. It featured Saturday afternoon serials. Legend had rats running across the stage, and friends hitting them with large red marbles stolen from tin reflectors, a brief fashion over headlights on cars. As it was, there were two safer movie houses, including the New Mary Lou, and a drive-in. The Old Mary Lou also folded.

In its block were the tough bars, where if you walked past, you might stumble into a fistfight crashing out the door. Don't ask me how such rumors started, but I always walked that block cautiously even on a weekday afternoon. Later the football coach, under whom I suffered sufficient embarrassment, renovated a store on that street and I felt slightly ill at ease just stopping by to visit. Still later, coming home with a friend from the university, we chose one of those bars for a few beers, with my brother, and with a slight spirit of adventure, my brother warning us again as we went inside.

A whorehouse stood near Scudder's junkyard. At least one was said to. Red light and all, though I never saw it. In my eagerness to believe, I reasoned they just stuck the red light out at night, switching bulbs on the porch. Walking past in daytime, which I seldom had reason to do, I never saw any indication of the place being other than shabby and private. Nor did I ever notice a red light when driving by at night.

Another difficult place was the Negro barbeque joint near their school. We never walked their streets as kids. When we drove, we learned them, four or six blocks, south of Eastwood and Conway, clustered as a black neighborhood, spilling down one side of a slope and crawling up another. One side was a ravine, the other more open, and the better of the through streets went there. The barbeque was on the second street, steeper and more pitted. As we dipped down and up again, we'd notice cars clustered around it, men coming in and out its screen door, the woodsmoke thickening. Blacks ate there, but white families knew to order slabs they'd take home. Eventually we stepped in ourselves, looking for someone we had played football with but didn't visit otherwise. We might even have a beer before we left.

Before we were quite of age, beer came more easily from Shelby Smith, Reverend Smith's daughter, cigarette-loving, buxom, and hearty, who tended Sarley's bar. Sarley's was the better bar and restaurant off the square, and we could come in the back door, from the alley, and get a six-pack from her. I think she always let our parents know and would refuse if they objected; apparently they did not.

EASTER

The Sunday school I attended—we mostly slipped out after that and left church to the adults, or to those in the choir—was off the northeast corner of the square. When we slipped away we'd go to a drugstore, ostensibly for a soda, but more to seek a few words with the girls, or to stand and thumb magazines, particularly nudist magazines, in black and white on cheap paper, and with small black bars striking out the eyes. Three other churches were within easy reach. The drugstore had reason to open Sunday mornings.

Easter, though, was different, being not just a holy day but the culmination. It was one of the two days in the year when we didn't leave after Sunday school. That morning greenery festooned the altar, with more branches and blossoms swelling each of the balcony pillars, and amid those blossoms birds sang. Canaries held forth from their cages, a dozen or more positioned around the sanctuary, caroling. Reverend Smith didn't seem to mind but read the Scriptures and delivered his sermon spiritedly, rising above the joyful noise. Shelby led the choir, her hair pulled back to a bun, its red sheen blending with her magenta robe, her voice doing as much as her father's to conduct the service.

There at the focal point of the service, many magnets were pulling—Shelby, Reverend Smith, and Carolie, who also sang in the choir—even the irrepressible pianist, to the canaries a dumpy but droll companion, and the director of the marching band at the State School behind Eastwood, who on less holy Sundays might play "Dixie" and "Yankee Doodle" simultaneously, one with his left hand, the other with his right.

They were waiting for me, not just for me, of course, but I felt particularly summoned. The whole of the season preceding, beginning imperceptibly after Christmas and building to this moment, leading through weeks of lessons detailing Joseph's selection and adornment, his being sold into Egypt, his exaltation there, his ministry to his brothers during the famine, then Moses, the plagues and the Exodus, the Children of Israel wandering the desert, the very landscape of Lent, which we didn't really follow except to cut back on sweets, then also the sense of Easter as a holiday coming, and a change of season, with preparations for dinner whether or not the family went to church, and something new bought for dress and for warmer weather—all this led to an early Sunrise Service, then to this heightened chance for entering communion. The Promised Land had been reached; the walls of Jericho were falling, and it was time to unburden my barricaded heart. But I kept to the balcony rather than venturing the spectacle of immersion, in that shallow tub off the altar to the left.

For others it came more naturally, perhaps. But my parents were not religious so had not encouraged me. My grandmother, who thought of herself as Quaker, who subscribed to and sometimes wrote articles for a magazine called *Prevent World War III*, a mushroom cloud on every cover, attended this church—there being no Meeting in town, and Reverend Smith being our neighbor—and she brought me along to Sunday school. But I was already of an age where I was supposed to make up my own mind, and as good as the story sounded, I wasn't convinced. It seemed worse to pretend a faith I didn't have, so I sat in the balcony and watched.

OLDER WOMEN

My grandmother lived with us. Two of her sisters lived nearby. When the younger died, my grandmother moved in with her remaining, older sister. My cousins' grandmother and her sister lived across the street. Carolie's grandmother lived with her, and an older couple with a single daughter older than my parents lived next door to us.

"Go visit the Staubs; they'll be glad to see you." Such was my mother's frequent urging, as if, and it seems to have been largely true, a few moments' direct contact with one of us growing up on the street was a gift of some importance. With my grandmother and great aunt, Mother's request was more emphatic. I was scheduled to visit them regularly. Another means was a "German lesson," the two women being bilingual. For fifteen minutes a day, but not every day, for several years, I sat down to bits of German with my grandmother. I memorized paradigms, copied lessons in a notebook, conversed a little, learned that angular German script.

Sometimes Grandmother forgot to put in her false teeth, and her mouth sagged like a hand puppet bowing. Her hearing aid didn't favor the lesson much either. Often she'd seem abstracted; that's when I'd notice the stacks of magazines and sheet music around her dark room. She had been an instructor of piano at a small women's college, meeting my grandfather in that town, a farm boy who played a light-hearted guitar. "Tante Magda" would be moving about the living room. She had cracked both hips and her back after turning eighty-five, was blind in one eye and not well sighted in the other. But she remained vigorous, pushing a walker around the house, doing most of the cooking, getting out her painting supplies—I remember a cannister of serious brushes, full like a vase of zinnias, and a palette of hardened, darkening oils.

She had lived as a painter, miniature portraits being her specialty in one period, still lifes in another. For a while, it had been still lifes arranged around oriental dolls. Now bent, short, and shrinking, her hair kept waist-length but in a bun and retaining hints of yellow, she dominated the house, kept a sheet over the sofa, or davenport as she said, kept her sister off stage center, and was far more outspoken and entertaining. "Would you let the Venetian blinds come live in your home?" she inquired, while showing me one item or another salvaged from Europe. The answer to her rhetorical question was that she would not, and I worried about her lack of charity. She also kept pressing Reverend Smith to take her dancing.

DEATH

In a small town with sufficient grandparents, deaths were common, but what I mostly remember are deaths by car. Traffic deaths disfigured my generation. One classmate's car went out of control on the east side of town, killing his sister. Another's went off a curve coming in from the south, killing the younger sister of another friend. We all knew the right front seat was the suicide seat, and, unless driving, we all jockeyed for it. A grade-school sweetheart's younger brother also died in a wreck. At least three more high-school classmates died on the highway soon after graduation.

Clarion, Iowa, 1973

Galena, Illinois, 1973

Bucyrus, Ohio, 1973

Lincoln Valley, North Dakota, 1968

Clarion, Iowa, 1974

Eldridge, North Dakota, 1972

Quinn, South Dakota, 1971

Harvard, Illinois, 1980

Washington, Missouri, 1974

Apache, Oklahoma, 1969

Geronimo, Oklahoma, 1969

Lanark, Illinois, 1969

Parkston, South Dakota, 1969

Saco, Montana, 1973

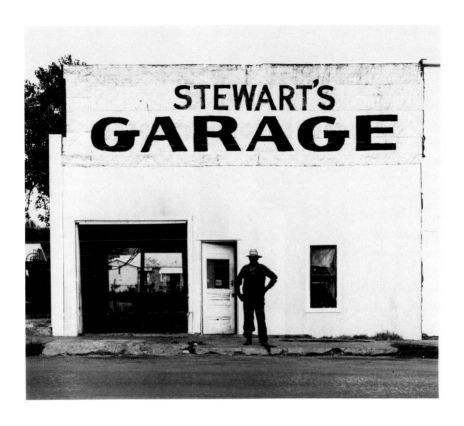

Cement, Oklahoma, 1969

Fayetteville, West Virginia, 1974

Wrecked cars were our memento mori. I remember being urged, one Sunday, to see a freshly wrecked car that had yet to be towed into town. We drove out to the crossroad where it sat, next to a wire fencerow, a sprinkling of mulberries, and acres of shimmering, dust-tinged corn, and stared at the twisted metal, the shattered windshield, the motor pushed back toward the driver's lap—at least he had been removed, but small pieces of flesh, mulberry-tinged, clung to the broken glass.

Marion found a more gaudy death several years later. Marion spent most of his high school years in reform school. When he returned, always briefly, he was an object of wonder, especially in the locker room, where he exhibited tattoos in unusual places. Later, he spent time in the penitentiary, and then rode with a group of motorcyclists. He died among them, and the story I heard was that they came to his funeral and sped over his grave, saluting him with pistols.

Perhaps that's just the movies, but I heard it said. The last time I saw Marion, he knelt mowing the sheriff's lawn. The jail, too, was just off the square, and I had paused before it at our single traffic light. Marion's back was to me while he edged a flowerbed. "Hey Marion, what ya doin'?" I called out. "Two years," he said, without even turning around.

The summer before our senior year, I spent two weeks pouring cement on those grain elevators that rose into the skyline compromising the courthouse. Once the pouring started, it had to proceed continuously so as not to create seams. Crews were needed around the clock. The elevators were mostly up by the time a few friends and I joined in, working a shift from eleven to seven. We pushed wheelbarrows of cement along plank runways over mesh-covered forms, or sorted and placed steel reinforcing rods.

OSHA would have shut the place down. We rode the cement bucket up and down to work, standing on its rim, between the steel cables that raised or lowered it, keeping our hands close to the running cables for an illusory sense of safety; we certainly couldn't grab them, but their position helped us gauge our balance. The bucket rim was about as wide as a piece of railroad track; we stood a little sideways on it, and so were hoisted a hundred feet or so off ground.

The night Marion came to work, he stood around below, patting his windbreaker pocket, asking people if they wanted to see what he had. He said he had a gun. Eventually he came up on top. But he never really got to work. The foreman wanted to see the gun and then wanted to take it, and Marion, unwilling to permit that, left. A shaggy pup of a story, but it's a persistent image— Marion standing with a few men atop an adjacent tower, their voices accenting the shadowy summer night, not angry but insistent, Marion turning and descending on the big bucket's rim. I noticed I was staring the courthouse dome dead on—it was a little past twelve—as I turned from watching him slouch away, toward a black girl's house, rumor had it.

Years later, when I searched out the grave of a close friend, one I had helped carry there, I found Marion's only a few steps away. Both had small, flat stones. Luther's just held his name and dates. Marion's featured further decoration, pistons crossed beneath a skull and the legend "Outlaws Forever."

LUTHER

L uther's death galvanized our high school. He was popular, a basketball player, doing well in what we called the "solid" courses, and had the flare of an artist. His family had lived along the ravine that edged the black neighborhood south of Eastwood but now lived on a scrap of land several miles south of town. I think his father worked as a farm laborer.

Approaching sixteen and not getting along with his father,

Luther found a job with a commercial sign-maker willing to foster his willingness to work and his artistic talent. Soon Luther had permission to stay in town and sleep at the shop. One October evening, he came to a j.v. football game driving the sign painter's truck. Luther's new patron decided he didn't want to be responsible for that and so sent Luther home. A phone call found Luther's father, who came into town. Frustrated and angry, Luther took a cab home instead. By the time his father got home again, Luther was dying on the living room floor of a self-inflicted wound from a .22 rifle.

The news came to most of us the next morning, to me, during the first period. There were already whispers in the hall, and Luther didn't take his seat next to Art and me in that geometry class. Our teacher hurried from the room and came back with the awful announcement. Art, Luther's best friend, went home instantly and stayed in seclusion all that day and the next. Three days later, he played the fiercest football game of his young life. The rest of us went through the day in an odd synthesis of grief, exhilaration, and trance. The announcement, never made general, seemed to skip from one class to another and flash into conflagration in the halls. We would hear outbursts of sobs from scattered places, then find huddles of schoolmates talking in hushed, urgent voices.

Then there was the vicarious thrill of our association with tragic life, our self-consciousness while monitoring differing reactions and discovering how to act. Cathy, Luther's steady girlfriend, stayed in the auditorium all day, crying copiously, with various friends venturing to learn around her how one gives comfort. For two days more we made pilgrimages to the funeral home across the street, to see a casket with someone other than a grandparent in it, to see Luther's body lying at rest, his square features a touch defiant, and with a lump on the side of his head. Many of us went more than once.

No one really knew his parents, except Art, and they seemed strangers at their son's funeral. It was a funeral for us; we fifteen- and sixteen-year-olds were the leading citizens that warm October morning, with the casket still open, the long line for viewing, the sobs again from the girls, as each person took her or his place beside the body. We stood there staring death in the face, and we were awed by it.

BEST FRIEND

In the year or so before Luther's death, I began to think of Art as my best friend, and after that tragedy our friendship deepened. He had a steady girl, as I did not, and was a far better athlete, a true all-arounder. We shared work, confidences, developed a sense of direction exploring ideas with each other, took most of the same classes. We forget, later on, how easy it was to talk at one time, intimate talk being boundless as prairie, as full of currents as our rivers. One late summer afternoon, either the summer before Luther died or the summer after, we were camping with several other friends in woods south of town. It was the last week before football practice, meaning early August. Corn was beginning to fire, the landscape browning off, the leaves on the scrub oaks beginning to crinkle before losing their green and so revealing their color. Somehow the other guys in our party went exploring, but Art and I stayed in camp, preferring the company of each other. We kept a fire smoldering and warmed a couple cans of C rations Art had salvaged from his older brother, who had been a paratrooper and then a smoke jumper in western forests. We each had a hatchet, and we sat astraddle an old softening log, as fat as horses might have been beneath us, and picked away at it while talking. I can't begin to remember what we spoke of—girls, cars, fear of death, football, friends, parents, ideas of God and of foreign places, hunches about college—but we kept it up all afternoon, stroking that log almost idly, reducing it to chips, doing the work of the next several winters and summers, and the talk just kept on talking. We found a reservoir that kept us fueled for years, if not finally for a lifetime, but with more than a little left in it that could still be tapped. Though by now the large ideas come harder.

BASKETBALL COACH

Unlike football and track, basketball was a sport for which you could not volunteer. Our coach would scout junior-high gym classes and, sidling up to a young man afterward, would say, "Son, what size shoes do you wear?" Thus, you were "invited out."

Never being selected, I spent four years as manager and statistician. I cleaned and polished the two dozen practice balls daily. I found the hole around a pipe at the top of the storeroom that gave me a cramped view of the girls' locker room. I swept the floor before practices, before games, and during halftime. I packed the trunks with uniforms and saw that they made the bus. Once I packed the keys inside a trunk and the A team had to wear the B team uniforms that were already sweaty. I kept shot charts, writing in the number of every player where he attempted a shot, circling it if good. I passed countless passes to awkward centers improving their hook and jump shots. And in my senior year, I was writing up the games, or games coming, almost daily for the town paper. I never thought to question the value of so serving my classmates and this trim, taciturn, dark-haired, hawk-featured man, who, we heard, had been a champion hurdler in college.

He kept things simple and usually won. He always had a guard who could penetrate and a sturdy forward or two for rebounds.

His best player, the guard with the effortless jump shot, was the son of a colleague who taught shop. His team made free throws, two-hands, underhanded. It attacked the zone from the baseline after quick passes. He never panicked when behind, never raised his voice or betrayed excitement. His calm, in the last minute or so, probably helped his team pull many games out. Once we were down five points with five seconds on the clock and won; but caving in to the tension and intending to ease defeat by readying things inside, I went ahead into the locker room, only to be surprised some long moments later by the teams' shouts. Then there would be the long bus ride home with a stop at the drive-in. Carolie and the other cheerleaders would already be there in their urgent red sweaters, making the place feel Mediterranean in its abundance. Coach would stand at the door and peel off dollars for us from a wad in his pocket. It looked an impressive bundle, a dollar for each of us, enough for a burger, fries, shake, and small change.

In my last two years I began to scout other teams as well as keep records on our own. At tournaments, Coach would keep me with him to watch a second game and to keep a chart on it. Then we'd drive home in his Olds 88, a car more modern and powerful than my parents', skimming the hills and curves in the winter quiet, the cold-looking stars making a shot chart of the heavens on a shot-happy night, the sight of the courthouse dome coming just in time to keep me from nodding off. We must have conversed—"that old peckerwood," he'd say about a player, or maybe a father—but I can't remember what our subjects were, and I remember very little of what he said, except once in a class in state history when he advised us that smoking was like tossing a quarter out the window daily.

He was looking out the window, no doubt. He taught that whole class looking out the window, or at the floor. And in our time, he never invited out a black. I never questioned it then but think I remember Art expressing, quietly, a stifled sense of justice. Eugene, Walter, and several others all played football and ran track. Any one of them might have been a player. If so, we never found out. Their presence wasn't yet complete enough in those first years of integration for anyone to pursue the matter.

On trips home now, I run across Coach at a farm sale or county fair. Or I've seen him joining a crowd of older men for morning coffee in a cafe on the square. The one time I made a point of greeting him, our conversation stumbled as I would have in drills. Since then I've let him pass, and given the habits of his eyes, I can't be sure he's noticed.

REUNION

High school casts a large shadow over a small town and over the memory of its people, perhaps because it is really meant to convey us into adulthood. Graduations after it are anticlimactic. In a town not given to the professions, full-time work comes early and adulthood and puberty crowd closely together. Rumor had one-tenth of my graduating class standing pregnant on the stage. Several girls were already married and probably twice a tenth had husbands by the end of that summer. Not quite half of us went on to college and another fair fraction to the service. Almost everyone had a job of some kind, and for many the shift to working full days was barely perceptible. Some simply stopped taking the bus in from the country. Farmers, mechanics, grocers, truck drivers, shop clerks, small-factory workers, local entrepreneurs, inheritors of one small business or another—many classmates found college inessential.

And so was our reunion. Oh, reunions are erratic events, I

know. The first one I made was my twenty-fifth. For it, classmates and a scattering of other friends came from a range of places, including both coasts, but many who'd stayed around town didn't join us. Perhaps their interlocking memories had become too baroque as scenes of youth merged with those of succeeding years, or maybe just too clouded. The afternoon of the reunion, I found a very early girlfriend running a Casey's store. Once we had played George and Martha Washington in a grade-school pageant, our selection riveting the class, since we were taken to be sweethearts. Much later, as seniors, she had run up in the hall to show me her engagement ring the day she got it. And I had looked her up when I came back to town for the reunion, but she didn't come to the dance. Perhaps she and others were shy of bringing their lives to the party which, if so, is a shame, because few were showing off. My brother, who has stayed in town himself and gone to all his reunions, says the posturing slows down radically after the tenth. But many of us gathered to enjoy drinks, dinner, and dance, and a picnic the next day in the park. A group photo placed class officers in the middle once more, even though a mostly new set had displaced us in practice, doing the real work of bringing us together.

We entered a charmed circle, bountiful for its moment. I'd driven six hours to attend and knew one man coming from a town only a half hour from where I started. We met pleasantly but had made no move to travel together, or now to visit once we got back. And, living right off Interstate 80, I invited several classmates known to travel east and west to stop with us, knowing they probably would not.

Still it was a good party. Two women chastized me for not dancing with them enough; and one, whom I just could not recognize though we'd shared classrooms from the second grade on, might have been secretly pleased—she'd lost thirty pounds preparing for the party.

BARBARA

R ecently a friend saw me standing at a university bulletin board, studying the notice of an academic conference. "You should offer a paper," she came over to encourage, "it's a good conference." Having gone to the host school, she knew its organizers.

"Well, at least it's close to home."

"Where's that?" she asked, surprised, and I said. She replied she came from the same town, had gone to my high school—our high school—graduating eight years after I did. But our accidental meeting gave us small means of reunion, for she knew none of my names and I none of hers. Oh, she knew the coach, knew he had learned to "ask out" some blacks, and she knew my two classmates who had returned to teach in our school. But she didn't know of Walter or Eugene, no great surprise. She didn't know of Carolie or Art. She didn't know of Marion or Luther. She didn't know of Carolie's quarterback, who had at least got a scholarship to the state university, or of the guard Carolie married, who starred at West Point. She didn't know of the runner who went into electronics with NASA. Though a musician herself, she didn't know of the pianist who introduced us to "Weekend Monitor"—to Chris Connor, Bob and Ray, and Ella Fitzgerald—who has his own divider in most record stores now and is on "Weekend Monitor" occasionally himself. She didn't know of Elaine, who sang with the pianist. She didn't know of our science whiz who went to college on a merit scholarship, became absorbed in Scientology, and dropped out. She didn't know any of the pantheon that had absorbed me completely only two high-school generations ahead of hers. Barbara's memories and fixations must interlock as thickly as my own, yet are all but entirely different.

If You Can Talk
to a Guy

The waitress at the Village Inn Cafe in Winnebago, Minnesota, bounces back and forth between our booth in the very back of the café and a round table in the front window occupied by three women and two men, all nursing their coffee. It is four o'clock and the Village Inn is almost empty, its regulars back home, cooling off in front of fans—their morning and afternoon coffees, their gossip of adultery, cancers, trips to Arizona, and farm foreclosures behind them. It might have been on a day like this, around two o'clock in the afternoon, that Harold Golly met up with Henry Dauner at the counter of the Village Inn, over coffee and lemon meringue pie. They were neighbors, Henry's farm just across the fields from Harold's, and had worked together often, combining one or the other's corn in the fall. For several years, as Harold tells the story, Henry's health had been bad. Then his wife had died of breast cancer. After that, Henry had decided to sell his farm. And he was planning to sell it to Harold's daughter and son-in-law. Everything had been agreed on since January.

Henry had first talked about selling the farm a year and a half earlier. One morning, as soon as he got the crops in that spring, Henry had stopped over at Harold's. "I just don't feel like farming anymore," he said. Then he drove away. That was on a Friday, Harold remembers, and as usual his daughter Mary and her husband, Duane, were due in from Minneapolis, where they were both teachers. That night at supper, while the family passed the corn from Harold's garden and the beef from his herd of Angus, Harold stopped chewing for a moment and looked around the table, from his wife, Helen, to Mary, and then to Duane. "Henry says he's going to sell his farm," he told them. "He doesn't feel like farming anymore."

Mary put down her fork and looked straight at her father. "You go back and tell Henry we'd like to buy it."

That fall, probably on a late-October morning, the air papery cool, Harold drove down the lane away from his house—past the grove of bur oaks and the apple orchard, over the small creek, down the county road, so windy even the natives give directions in left and right, rather than the traditional north and south, and finally across the one-lane bridge that had collapsed several times the winter before—to help Henry harvest his last crop of feed corn. Neither man mentioned the imminent sale of the farm.

A few months later, in December, Harold noticed Henry in his driveway one morning, and went out to meet him. "Do you think Mary and Duane still want the farm?" Henry asked, the window on his pick-up cranked down halfway, his breath pluming up in front of his face. "I think so," Harold answered. "I'll call them tonight."

"Well," Henry said, "if they want it, tell them to meet me at the attorney's office in Truman on Saturday."

So they met in Truman—Henry, Duane, Mary, and the attorney—and they agreed on everything. That Monday, Mary and Duane returned to finish out their year in Minneapolis and Harold and Henry chatted, as usual, over coffee at the Village Inn. Outside, the snow drifted in the ditches, and the windows of the café frosted up so that you could no longer see across the street to the filling station. Over the next few months, the bridge leading to

Harold's house collapsed two more times. The pipes in Henry's barn burst. And just outside of town, a couple from Joplin, Missouri, lost their orientation during a blizzard and froze to death in their car.

But by June, the county had begun work on a new bridge and Duane and Mary were getting ready to move, packing up their books and organizing a garage sale to clear out their daughter's old toys, the green easy chair the cat had shredded with its claws, and kitchen odds and ends—old jelly glasses, an extra grater or two, a one-legged colander, their first set of dishes.

One day that June, right before Mary and Duane were due in town, Harold stopped at the Village Inn after a round of golf. When he walked in, he saw Henry sitting at the counter. Harold tipped his seed cap to Kathy the waitress, then walked over to where Henry was sitting and straddled the stool next to him. They talked as usual—about Harold's golf game, about last week's storm that had knocked over half of Jim Nelson's corn. But Harold noticed that Henry was very quiet. "It was a beautiful June day," Harold recalls. "And when we finished our coffee, we walked out and stopped at one of our pickups. Tears began to roll down Henry's cheeks and off his nose."

"I can't sell Duane and Mary the farm the way I want to," Henry said. "I gotta have more money down or the judge won't approve the sale."

"Well," Harold said, "Henry, now don't get downhearted about this. Let me go home and talk to Helen. We'll help buy it, I think."

Harold and Helen did help Duane and Mary buy the farm. And when we visited Harold's place, last summer, sent there by some friends in neighboring Blue Earth who thought we might enjoy both Harold and the view, Harold told us the story of the sale. "So, you see," he said, when he had finished, his hoarse voice rising, "that's the advantage of being able to talk to a guy face-to-face." Then, Harold lifted his head and raised his arm nose-high, his index finger pointing across acres of corn that wound their way up and down the hills and around the Blue Earth River banked on both sides by cottonwoods. "See that stand of trees over there, right at the end of my finger?" he asked, indicating a blur of green. "Well, that's Mary and Duane's farm, right behind those trees. And right over here," he pivoted his body ninety degrees to the east, "is my son Tom's farm. He farms that big corn field. Oh, he taught school for a while. But then his father-in-law decided to sell. And all Tom ever wanted to do was farm, anyway. I can show you his drill and planter. They're just out in the shed here."

When Harold Golly told Henry not to get downhearted on that beautiful June morning, when he told him he'd talk to Helen about helping to buy the farm, it's not likely that he planned to stop off at his lawyer's, or consult the *Minneapolis Star*'s farm section to check on the price of land. Nor is it likely that he rushed home, and finding Helen in the kitchen icing his favorite chocolate cake, asked her to put down her wooden spoon and listen. More likely, Harold went out and worked in his garden on that beautiful summer day, running his hoe up and down the rows of corn and tomatoes, bending over the cucumbers to weed, setting the hose next to the beets and letting the water seep into the blue-black earth as he worked. And once he had finished in the garden, pinching back several tomato plants, gathering the last of the summer's peas, he had probably gone back into the house and taken a shower. Then, he probably sat down with the newspaper, in his easy chair by the front door, to wait for Helen to call him to supper. And once they were sitting at the square table in the kitchen, with its plastic flowered cloth, his fork full of mashed potatoes, Harold probably said to Helen, "Ran into Henry at the Village Inn today."

"Oh," Helen might have replied, continuing to chew on her pork chop.

"Henry seemed sort of quiet."

"Well, he's had it kind of rough."

"The judge wants more money down for the farm. I told him we might help," Harold may finally have said, his fork clicking against the plate as he set it down.

People like Harold, Henry, and Helen communicate important things with few words. They act in the same way. And it's understandable. Their economy of gesture, paradoxically, conforms to the way they make their living. The scale of their lives is enormous—hundreds of acres, thousands of bushels of corn or soy. But once they prepare the fields and plant, they must step aside, leaving their fates to nature and the U.S. government. Even the way they plant signals economy. Harold and Henry don't broadcast their seed by the fistful. Instead, in the old days walking along the rows with a horse and drill, or today mounted atop twenty-four-row planters, they deposit at the most three kernels to a hill. And if later in the season the weather turns against them, bringing in enough lashing rain and wind to knock over entire sections of adolescent corn, they don't—like a vegetable gardener—throw on their boots and slickers and dash through the fields hammering in stakes and tying up the stalks. They sit by their radios and listen. And then, when the winds have subsided and the rains tapered off, they might go and stand at the top of a rise, one hand shading their eyes to survey the damage. And even then, even if they see half their corn lying on its side, the tassels buried in mud, they don't run to the barn for twine. Instead, they go back into the house and turn the radio on again, listening to the news, assessing the extent of the damage in the area, waiting. Any other response—hurried calls to neighbors, graphic descriptions of the storm or the state of the fields to family—would be an excess, not unlike the ten inches of rain and the sixty MPH winds of the recent storm.

By necessity, then, farmers are conservers; they save everything—seeds, old crates, junk cars down by the creek, string, buckets, work shoes. Words are no exception.

"Can I get you anything else?" the waitress at the Village Inn asks, approaching our table, her blond hair fanning out from her head as she walks. "Well, at least have another cup of coffee. I'm not used to people just having one cup," she urges, already leaning over to pick up our mugs and refill them from the glass pot steaming in her hands. We thank her and she smiles at us, displaying a set of teeth that look like kernels of white sweet corn. Then she twirls around and bounces back toward the cash register—just in case one of her two tables should suddenly ask for the bill. As she passes the group at the round table in the front, the thin, hollow-chested man with the hearing aid calls her over. The rest of the café is still empty, its newly Naugahyded booths shiny, the front counter, where Harold and Henry used to sit, updated to a series of tables for two, making the café feel truncated and incomplete.

"Do you play sports in school?" the man asks the waitress.

"Yes. I played volleyball last year," she answers, flexing the muscles in her arms. "And this year I'm planning to go out for cheerleading."

"I thought so," the skinny man replies, and everybody at the table nods in agreement.

"Why don't you try basketball?" the second man asks, shifting his weight in the chair so that his belly rests on his left instead of his right knee. "That's a good sport these days. Always has been, of course."

The conversation at the front table gradually peters out and the waitress busies herself behind the counter. A while later, a raspy voice drifts toward us: "You're from out of town, aren't you?" We look up and the skinny man, his glasses too large for his face, beckons us over. "Well, so are we. We come from Bricelyn, the next town over. Population 285. We're out for the afternoon," he explains.

"Yes," a high, quavering voice joins in. "Our sister's at the home here and we come once a week to take her out and give her a little break. We always come to the Village Inn."

"Yes, we always come to the Village Inn," the woman in the middle, the oldest, whispers. "And they've just remodeled this past year."

We look around at the straight-back metal and plastic chairs, the chandelier at the entrance, the indoor–outdoor carpet on the floor, green with yellow diamonds, the same green as Harold Golly's carpet, but his covered a living room floor that had been laid in 1900.

O f course, Harold's house hadn't always stood on the crest of the hill, next to the grove of bur oaks, Harold had told us that afternoon. The original farm house had burned down, and this one, built by the White brothers, two carpenters living on an adjacent farm, had been moved all the way from Huntley in 1911. One of Harold's friends, a neighbor on another adjacent farm, had seen it all happen. In fact, he had helped. The man's name was Bob Hope, and he had been seventeen years old at the time. He was the person responsible for moving the plank from behind the rollers every two hundred feet, when the cable the horses had been winding in ran out.

"It was quite an operation," Harold said. "They attached cables to the house, and a team would go round and round and round, winding the cable until they got the house up to this jack. Then they had to unstake that and take it out another two hundred feet. It took them a few days, what with the rain and the cables breaking. And I think one of the horses even collapsed."

When Harold finished telling the story, we looked over the fields in the direction of Huntley, west of Winnebago, up and down five miles of sinewy road, and imagined the two-story, white-frame house with its front porch being towed across the prairie. It would have been in the fall—the winter field snowed in, the spring field mud, the summer field full of corn—in the fall, after the corn was picked, the wind slapping the leaves in the trees, the cows gleaning the stubble. But as Harold told the story that afternoon, we could tell that for him, the house was moved again and again, whenever he looked out over his fields toward Huntley—Bob Hope, the White brothers, the team of horses, their driver, Harold's in-laws who had lived in the house first, all still present, too.

Each time Harold Golly steps out of his house and looks across his land, east to his son Tom's, west to Mary and Duane's, all of these people assemble there, on the crest where he stands. And that afternoon as he told us his stories, we had felt a part of that assembly also, looking out over the fields with Harold and Helen and their granddaughter Kristen, their pasts and presents coming together on a piece of land and at a time that transcended last year's winter blizzards, the spring floods, the summer's oats ripening next to Harold's garden, to create an eternal moment, outside of time and space.

"Why don't you pull up a chair?" the skinny man in the Village Inn invites. And before we have even scooted into place, he asks, "Where did you say you were from again? We're from Bricelyn."

"Yes, they come and take me out every week," the oldest woman whispers, "my two sisters and my brothers-in-law."

"Yes," a third female voice adds, "We used to be five sisters. Two died, so now there's just the three of us. We come up from Bricelyn. We all live there. Well, except for my sister, here, who's in the home. See," she continues, pulling a pin the size of a half-dollar out from her dress and craning her neck down to read the "I love Bricelyn" logo.

"What are you girls doing here?" the skinny man asks.

We tell him we are there to interview gardeners for a book we are writing.

"Then you oughta go talk to my next-door neighbor, Leroy Nelson. Everyone calls him Doc. He's a retired veterinarian. He's a real gardener."

"Boy, does he have melons!" the youngest sister smacks her lips.

"Oh, yeah. And he even raises his seedlings inside in the winter," says the skinny man, shoving his glasses back up his nose. "But the funniest thing is, Doc just raises the stuff to give away. He has another huge garden somewhere out in the country, and you should see him in August. He loads up his pickup with melons and drives up and down the streets of Bricelyn giving them away. And then he takes another load up to his daughter in Winona. And another to his son in the Cities. My God, he even gives his seedlings away. He raises a thousand of them in his basement and gives a lot of those to Harold Beckman in the spring. And Harold's another one. He goes around Bricelyn planting trees. He used to manage the canning factory over there and when he retired he decided to beautify the town. Made a planter for petunias at the entrance to our city park. And a few years back, he put in a whole row of Austrian pines. And then last year, he had a big barbeque for the town, a fund-raiser (he raised $975.00), so he could plant another row of pines at the north edge of town as a snow break. And Maureen— she owns the beauty shop—is quite a gardener herself. Of course, I garden some. Mostly tomatoes. But this year's been a bad year. You're welcome to stop by, though."

The three sisters and the one brother-in-law nod their agreement.

"Maybe we'll give Leroy a call," we say, and ask the waitress for the pay phone.

"When you call Doc, just tell him Leon Lora sent you. He's my neighbor. Lives right next door to me. Right on Fifth and Elm. Just across from the funeral home." Again everybody at the table nods and smiles, the oldest sister wiping her mouth with a lipstick-smeared napkin.

Back at our booth, we discuss whether or not to call Leroy Nelson. If we do call, we'll have to see him and his garden immediately, since we are planning to head back home that evening. And we are tired. We left Ames, Iowa, at 7:00 in the morning, driving straight north to Blue Earth, where we had an appointment with a woman who gardened and raised rabbits. Her garden turned out to be full of weeds, but she was very eager to brew up some Lipton tea and model her angora toe-warmers, mittens, and berets, the whole time telling us about her three sons' electronics business in San Diego and her daughters' recipes for rabbit and onion pies. After that, we barely had time to gulp down a cartonful of yogurt, sitting on the tailgate in front of the Blue Earth County Courthouse, before rolling up and down the tree-lined lane to Harold Golly's, where he, his wife, Helen, and granddaughter Kristen waited for us on the swing set in front of the house.

But somehow, we hate to let Leon Lora down. In the first place, he listened to us when we spoke. Not just politely or perfunctorily, but attentively. And then he responded, not with his own expertise, but with a list of people he thought might help us out. We don't always encounter listeners like that, our everyday lives populated by people from universities. And it feels good to be listened to. It's the way a red-tailed hawk must feel when the temperature is just right and it catches a thermal, and wings outstretched, it glides and glides, over a canopy of willows by the river, past a field of beans, over some pastureland where a few herefords loll around the watering tank, their tails swishing. A friend of ours from New York said he had never finished a sentence until he went to Iowa to study. "It was the first time anybody ever listened to me," he told us.

We also can't bear to let Leon down because he offered us small-town hospitality, inviting us into the web of social relationships that make up his world: his tomatoes, Doc Nelson's melons, his sister-in-law's illness, Bricelyn's history. And he would certainly learn if we ignored his invitation. All he'd have to do is walk next door. So, we open the *Rand McNally Road Atlas*, locating Winnebago, on the south-central border of Iowa and Minnesota, then, tracing our way back through Blue Earth over Interstate 90, we follow Highway 253 to Bricelyn. It's right on our way home.

We finger the map and calculate the mileage on the most direct route down the Faribault County roads. Harold Golly had been a county commissioner once, when he was sixty-two years old. For only one term, though, since the job had kept him away from home two-thirds of the time and—more important, he chuckled—it had interfered with his golf. During the four years he had served, there were the usual problems with welfare and pay raises, but Harold had boasted that afternoon that in all those four years, only one man had ever gotten mad at him. It was over a ditch. In the northeast part of the county, the land is flat and the ditches fill up with trees and dirt, creating a drainage problem, Harold explained. After several nights of open discussion, the commission had taken a vote on cleaning up some of those ditches.

Harold's had been the deciding vote. But according to Harold, he had been cornered. "One commissioner lived along the ditch in question, so he couldn't vote. And another sat talking in the back of the room all night and didn't come up and take care of his job. So, that left three of us to handle it—the chairman and two others. There were about one hundred seventy-five people there, and the other commissioner made the motion to clean the ditch. Well, I seconded it. And the chairman called for the vote. And there were just the two of us, so it passed!"

That was on a Tuesday night, and the man who got mad at Harold wasn't at the meeting. But on Thursday night, as Harold told it, when he went bowling, "Boy, that guy jumped all over me."

"You're gonna flood the ditch I'm on."

"Were you at the meeting the other night?" Harold asked.

"No. But I heard what you did. You're gonna clean out number three and that'll flood nine."

So Harold looked hard at the man—past the smoke from the man's cigarette curling up in front of his face, past the angry brown eyes and the scar stretching from his eyebrow to temple, where a scythe had caught him when he was just a kid—and asked, "Well, were you satisfied with what they did in 1948?"

"Yeah, that was fine," the man answered.

"Well, if you'd have been to the meeting, you'd know that all we're doing is cleaning the ditch to the same depth it was back in 1948, with the same slant on the bank."

"Well," the other man said, stubbing his cigarette out on the floor, "that's all right."

"So you see," Harold paused, adjusting his seed cap on his head, "if you can talk to a guy, you can generally take care of anything."

And by now, we think we understand what Harold meant by talking. In Winnebago, Minnesota, at least, talking doesn't mean analyzing. It doesn't mean taking a problem and dissecting it, then examining it through a series of lenses, philosophical, emotional, economic, sociological, and historical. Talking doesn't mean engaging in repartee, rationalizing, casting off guilt, blame, or insecurities, the way we might shed coats and sweaters on a warm spring day. For Harold Golly, and for the rest of the rural Midwest, talking means telling stories—stories about hailstorms and tornadoes, about stomach cancer and repossessions, about hired hands and chocolate cakes, about church potluck socials and college degrees.

So Harold Golly recalled the incident with his accuser as a story, as an event that became much larger than the five minutes they had spent together and the several sentences they had exchanged. Instead, it was a plot, set both in the bowling alley and the county courthouse, a plot that began with the first of three public discussions and ended in the Winnebago Bowling Alley, against the hum of the balls down the lanes and the crash of the pins onto the slick floor.

And if Harold recalls his life as a fabric of stories, with its warp and woof of family, farm, and town, and not as a yellowish, narrow band of ticker tape announcing a parade of achievements, he recounts his life as a story also. Any particular happening or sight—an ear of corn, a year-old steer attempting to mount its mother, a dead limb on an oak tree—may spark Harold, leading him and his listeners away from the moment, away from the green crest where his house sits looking over Elm Creek, away from the fields of corn, their tassels spraying out pollen in the wind, to the time his son Tom got trapped inside the corn bin, or to his own wedding day in the Presbyterian church next to the Interstate Building, the gladiolas around the pulpit from his mother-in-law's garden.

"Here's your bill," the waitress at the Village Inn says, ripping a piece of green paper from her pad. "No hurry, though. I'm just getting organized for the dinner crowd."

But it's time for us to be going if we're to stop and visit with Leroy Nelson, so we gather our money and equipment up and go to the register to pay, stopping to chat for a few more minutes with the Bricelyn crowd. Then we're rolling down Main Street, through Winnebago, and on to Highway 169. The day is just cooling down and the rising wind rushes through the truck and whisks the maps off the dash. We roll the windows up partway, our skin unbracing in the moist evening after an hour of air conditioning.

A half hour later we're driving through Bricelyn's downtown.

A few children ride bicycles up and down the sidewalk, on the east. And one block of boarded-up buildings stands on the west. There's a beauty shop, Maureen's Curling Corner, a lumberyard, a post office of blond brick with an American flag flapping out front, and a pink stucco veterinary office. But Regis Implement has gone out of business, as have the Variety Store, the grocery store, and the filling station at the end of the block. Bricelyn is clearly on its way down, and yet when we get out of the truck and walk over to the park to inspect Harold Beckman's petunia planter, we wonder if its citizens see the town the way we do. A new flower planter and a row of three-foot Austrian pines are the town's way of throwing a line out to the future. And the past is still present also, surfacing whenever anybody looks at Maureen's Curling Corner and remembers Trudy Oster, the first owner, with her tight blond curls, her rose-red Revlon shaping her lips into a heart, and her stories, told while her fingers wound the plastic rollers up the women's hair, then repeated by her customers at the supper table that night, and again over the backyard cannas the following afternoon.

In years to come, the stories in Bricelyn will likely be about Harold Beckman, and how the former canning-plant manager finished his life beautifying the town. And Harold Golly's descendants are likely to tell stories about how he combined until he was ninety years old, driving the machine one fall for twelve days straight. With their stories, the people of south-central Minnesota live in a fluid time and place, which allows them to see through boarded-up buildings to their future city park, splashed pink and red with petunias and set off by a grove of fifty-foot Austrian pines, their needles glossy, their dark gray bark cracked into deep hollows. It allows their worlds to be peopled not only by their husbands and wives, children and grandchildren, but also by the hired hand who lived on the farm twenty years earlier, or by an elementary-school friend who went off to live in the Twin Cities. And it allows their space to expand, almost indefinitely, to encompass their daughter's farm, three miles away, where their granddaughter is riding her bike up and down the gravel drive, to encompass even Japan, home of the exchange student who lived with their son the past year and graduated from Winnebago High School that spring.

Harold Golly and his friends live a kind of paradox. They are people of few words and gestures, their speech like the act of shucking peas, as they slip their planters' thumbs up the pod until four or five peas pop out. But many of them are also tellers of stories, twentieth-century bards, who feel equally at home with grander gestures—harvesting one thousand bushels of corn in one day, or inviting you into their homes for lemonade and an afternoon of stories, which can lead you anywhere, from the creek running along the farm to the hailstorm of 1907. Tall tales, if you didn't know them to be true. These are Harold Golly and his friends' conversation. Their form of recreation. They are what enables them to make it through the hail and the rain, the cancer and the senility, the bankruptcy and repossession. They are their blessing.

Grandma's Backbone, Dougie's Ankles

At one time or another, we all have to explain our lives to ourselves. We do this by remembering, and then by telling the story. Unfortunately, this is easier said than done. The story must be true to all of the multifarious details of our lives, while also being intelligible. If this does not sound utterly impossible to you, I hope you receive it as an assignment someday. You will find that when you try to relate everything, the result is boring. Any drama your life might possess is smothered under a meaningless succession of anecdotes. If you try to solve that problem by settling on a clever plot line, the drama gets better but the truth suffers. The tale takes on a life of its own, and all the strange occurrences that make you really you get suppressed. You become nothing more or less than the product of your own imagination.

What is the answer? I wish I knew. It appears, as my mother says, that we just have to do the best we can. Recently, I have been toying with the idea that my life can be explained as a battle between two places, places of big sense and places of little sense. I think I am a product, on the whole, of places of little sense. I am, however, fascinated by the wiles of the big sense. Let me try to explain.

I teach religious studies at Iowa State University, and have done so for six years. Iowa, by and large, is a place of little sense. Do not confuse such places with places of no sense, or of nonsense. Places of little sense have very much sense; it is just of a modest, local, sort: farmers in orange feed caps discussing whether the girls' basketball team hadn't oughta switched to five-player rules, doughnut makers showing sixteen-year-olds how to boil potatoes to make broth for Page's Bakery cinnamon rolls, children encouraged by their parents on Saturday night to lay out their Sunday clothes. Such people have a good deal of practical wisdom, knowledge located in bones and bellies.

I have not always been an Iowan. I grew up in the suburbs of the largest midwestern city, and studied for a good long time at the University of Chicago. Those are places of big sense. You do not see bumper stickers in Hyde Park saying "HUNGRY? EAT YOUR FOREIGN CAR!" You see personnel managers spending Tuesday mornings trying to find ways to cut sick-leave losses, philosophers spending their lives searching for the key to all moralities, dinner guests telling intimate details about the lives of G. E. Moore and Paul Tillich. There is plenty of knowledge here, of a cerebral sort. Often, the bones are brittle.

My introduction to the University of Chicago was a speech by an internationally renowned professor of religion. He informed a group of us entering graduate students—gathered for what we thought would be a few low-key comments—that we ought to be planning to publish books and become famous. If we were not, then we were probably in the wrong place. I looked around and saw nothing but young futurely famous authors. I wondered what I was doing there.

I made it through that place of big sense, and arrived at Iowa State to teach religion. This is not the University of Chicago. We are a small fish in the big pond of the sciences and humanities, and we are very self-conscious about this. We do not tell our students to get famous or get out. We tell them, as our most recent slogan has it, that "Iowa State Means Business." Like the farmers of my grandpa's generation who used to introduce themselves as "just farmers," we are preoccupied with the perception of our own mediocrity. When I graduated from Chicago, a professor informed me that I was going to a third-rate university. Since I have been here, I have heard unending arguments that we are second, not third.

My professor's assessment was balanced by my mother's. When I told her I had gotten the job, she said I was going home. She grew up on a farm near Mason City. Mom figured that Ames was as close to heaven as one could muster in this life. I figure Jack Kerouac must have been right: home is on the road, somewhere between Illinois and Iowa.

There are lots of things in my university—as there are lots of things in my life—that I do not understand. Iowa State is a land grant school, which means it is funded by taxpayers' dollars. As a result, it is a thoroughly secular institution. (This year the president did away with the Christmas-tree-lighting ceremony. Too Christian. The tree is still there, and the lights are on, but no one officially threw the switch. I have heard it said that Virgil the janitor did it.) Why do you teach religion at a secular university? Because someone has decided to pay you to do it. Well, then, how do you do it? You do the best you can.

Secular universities are supposed to be very liberal places. That is why we allow religion teachers on campus; we have classes in "Food Purchasing" and "The Philosophy of Leisure and Recreation," so why not "Bible"? Teaching religious studies here, I have become very conscious of the limits of liberalism. Universities, we proudly proclaim, are places where anything that can be thought may be thought, and anything that can be said may be said. The modern university protects diversity. You can be fired for disparaging remarks about women, blacks, or Jews. But try saying that there is a God, or that worship is a rational activity. You want to recommend that Christians who believe in creationism should have their diplomas revoked? It is done here in the campus newspaper by full professors. You want to denounce Iranians for practicing *jihad*, holy war? Bars hang signs over their doors saying "Iranians not welcome," and no one notices.

Teaching religion at state-funded schools is a touchy subject. Our program is cloistered in the Philosophy Department, where talk about religion can be closely guarded. Fortunately, many philosophers have escaped the prejudices of the broader university. Most of my colleagues have grown accustomed to people talking as if prayer meetings and kosher diets really made sense. They are not actively opposed to discussion of particular rituals and traditions. Nonetheless, they do come from places of big sense; some of them are trying to devise universal moral systems and to justify claims about ethical facts. As a consequence, they are constantly tempted to explain places of little sense—cafés in rural Iowa, Orthodox synagogues, Quaker Meetings—in terms of their own, bigger tradition. They call that tradition, somewhat immodestly, Reason.

Reason is liberal, and wants to be fair to the little places, but its tolerant superego always competes with its aggressive id. John Rawls, the Harvard philosopher, instructs us to make moral decisions by first separating ourselves from our places of little sense, drawing a "veil of ignorance" over our eyes, forgetting the particular memories, hopes, desires, and places that make us who we are. The German philosopher Jurgen Habermas aspires to have all ethical judgments made in the "ideal speech situation," a no-place where people would be free of the interests and aspirations that constitute individual identity. Kurt Baier insisted long ago that the only moral point of view was that of places of big sense: detached, objective, free of any allegiance to particular tribes.

If modern philosophy is ambitious, priding itself on big theories, it is also insistent on unwavering intellectual open-mindedness. This is its defense against those who object to its imperialistic tendencies. You do not like our single theory of all morality? That is all right, because we are always willing to listen tolerantly to opposing views. That sounds terribly nice, but there is a flip side here too. As people of little sense have pointed out to me, the problem with having too open a mind is that your brains may fall out.

We should not try to explain places of little sense. There is no General Theory of Little Places into which each particular Iowa county, farm community, or religious sect can be fit. How do we talk about such places? By telling stories about them, one by one.

My great-grandfather, Charles Williams Pippert, farmed 160 acres of little Iowa land for three decades. He was known as a man with a good deal of little sense, and as somebody who savvied horses. I have heard that he could make the rankest of nags lie down, roll over, and beg for cookies. He was asked once what it was that made him so adept at taming horses.

My great-grandpa, never one for straight answers, just muttered: "Aw, I dunno. I'm just an old farmer."

But one time he was pressed to be more specific about the source of his skill. He did not answer with a "Philosophy of Horse Handling," as the experts at my university now do.

He said, simply, "I know horses."

And what was it, exactly, that he knew about horses?

"Each horse is different," he replied.

Each place of little sense is different, and the difference makes a difference. To figure out such a place, you have to go there and listen. After hearing how people talk, you might begin to pick up a few commonalities. Then again you might not. If it seems that the people are tending to talk about how much snow they have had, and whether a hot summer means a cold winter, you had better listen a while longer. Before long they might be talking about John Rawls and Jurgen Habermas.

Now, a few of my colleagues have retained quite a little sense. They tend not to call themselves "modern" philosophers, but "postmodernists," or feminists, or narrativists. People like Richard Rorty, Carol Gilligan, and Stanley Hauerwas all exhibit a healthy skepticism about big sense. There is even an economist, believe it or not, E. F. Schumacher, who believes that small is beautiful, and who wants to scale back big-boned multinational businesses. Yet these people are exceedingly rare, not only in the boardroom but in the quadrangle.

Why? I think it is due to the level of coercion used in getting people to talk and think Reasonably. Young folk seeking admission to the business or university or agricultural guild are not told, "Here is the way we talk. You must talk this way as well." It would be much easier to resist if it were this forthcoming. But actual tactics are much more effective. The message is circulated subconsciously: "This is the *only* way for rational people to speak. If you do not follow suit you will not be invited to dinner." The message is no less clear for being so subtle. Objectivity and uncommittedness are not virtues that are to be recommended to the young; they are the very price of admission.

So much for all the rhetoric about universities being places where anything that can be thought may be thought. As I said before, these can be very intolerant places, where young farm women are trained in Colleges of Agriculture to repeat, "Farming is not a way of life; it is a *business*." They are places where white Lutheran seminarians presume to correct the black South African theologian Alan Boesak when he proclaims that tortured blacks will continue to fight apartheid "until the Lord comes again." The seminarians say knowingly, "If he really understood that conservative doctrine of the Second Coming, he would not use it." As if white men in Des Moines knew better than blacks living under apartheid what it means to trust in Jesus' return.

Such B.S., big sense, must be resisted. But how can a suburban boy respond? How do you hold together a Chicago Ph.D. and a Mason City farm in one story? You do the best you can. Iowa is a good place for that. Perhaps it is because the winters are so long, or the TV reception so bad, or the fact that there is so little besides farming and writing to do here, but Iowans tell stories. And for as long as the tale lasts, nothing else matters; there is peace on earth. The narrator pulls a plug out of our big toes; we sink and bend together, our bones, bellies, and brains meeting as we give ourselves to once upon a time.

In my beginning was Wheaton, Illinois. I grew up there in a two-bedroom house at 108 S. Chase St. It was Mom and Dad and Uncle Wes and Gordie, me, Dawn, Doug, and Wes' black lab, Bow, who lived in a wooden doghouse Dad built in the carport. My mother says these were the happiest years. We stayed that way by heading regularly for Grandma and Grandpa's farm. Crossing the Mississippi River, we would feel ourselves drawing upright as we entered cow country. Surprisingly, the state of sheep and hogs has a refreshingly sweet odor. It smells like milled corn, just like my Grandpa's gloves on Thanksgiving Day. But this is not vacation country. Just inhaling the air straightens your backbone, narrows your eyes. Perhaps it is the violent snowstorms. Or the violent rainstorms. Uncle Harold, who now farms Grandma and Grandpa's place, says the weather gets your dander up.

On this particular trip, Doug was in the back of our '54 Chevy, harmlessly twanging the rope that stretched across the back of the front seat. Dawnie was looking out the window; Gordie and I were screaming at each other, wrestling, occasionally bumping the back of my father's head. Dad, who is normally as irritable as a frozen fish, thought he heard all four of us wailing in his ear. He pulled the car to the shoulder.

"OK. That's it. Everyone line up behind the car," he said gently.

"Everyone?" we all wondered silently. Dad was not usually so undiscriminating. But not to worry; Dawn and Doug never got much anyway.

Gordie, the oldest, was always first.

"Grab your ankles," said my dad.

Gordie, his hair whipping in the Iowa breeze, stood defiant, erect. Until my father's belt whapped across his bottom. Then he swiftly grabbed his ankles, took his second lick, and strode back to the car.

I was next. I too could smell the corn and hogs, but I have always been the smartest of the kids. I whipped my back into an inverted U faster than you can say "Kiss your toes," grabbed my insteps, took my licking, and tripped off to join Gordie. Dawnie got her token slap—Dad upholding the pretense of justice—and then it was Doug's turn.

The baby, he was only five years old. His backbone was like mine, malleable as Play-Dough. We expected him to beat Dawn back to the car. But he did not. This particular afternoon, as the three of us sneaked astonished looks behind us, we saw that kid become an adult. Fiercely inhaling the country dust, there he stood, nearly upright, his hands rubbing only his thighs, occasionally reaching down no lower than his knees. We could not believe it. My father swatted him, yelling, "Grab your ankles!" Doug was stoic, unbending, not once going near his feet: innocent Daniel in the lion's den, David defying Goliath.

Finally it was over. My father had given up. Ordering Doug back into the car, Dad resumed his place at the wheel, and down the road we went. Mom was beside herself in confusion, and Doug was in tears. But we were awed. What a place this was! Just crossing the river had turned Doug into a man. "What grit! What courage! What a place!" our eyes said to each other.

People in places of little sense tell stories like this. While they last, the stories are their victory. They dwell in them; they do not

draw morals from them. Drawing lessons from stories is for philosophers. Being one, I cannot resist writing the next sentence.

There is a spiritual lesson about Iowa in Doug's story. It is this:
Iowa farmers are like Doug. They feel themselves caught in a
battle much bigger than they are. Even as they are taking their
beating, they see people sneaking astonished looks at them, rever-
ing them, making them into heroes. They see land values falling,
corn prices dropping, equipment purchases rising, interest rates
skyrocketing. They see fifty-five-year-old men going bankrupt.
They read about banks closing, Main Street businesses failing,
families breaking up. Suicide. And the farmers grimly hang in
there, standing almost upright. As a result, the media turn them
into cultural archetypes: the American Farmer, Modern-Day Hero.
But they are neither deceived nor consoled. These are men and
women of no nonsense; they see their battle in more real if humble
terms. For them, it is not a battle of the Humanizing Powers of the
Agrarian Tradition versus the Dehumanizing Powers of Industrial
Modernism. It is not a war of principalities and powers, the way
critics of modernity like Ellul and Rifkin draw it. It is a little fight
in this particular place, a very specific battle with the Federal Land
Bank, or the 1986 tax form, or a troublesome acre of button-
weeds.

Acknowledging the true, little sense of the farmer's struggle also
allows us to see more clearly its true significance. These are indi-
vidualized, local battles for this eighty acres purchased in anticipation of a son's joining the operation, for that crop of soybeans
damaged in the June hail, this John Deere tractor bought retail at
the wrong time.

When you are fighting your own little battles—as opposed to
Dan Rather's Big Battle—you know exactly what you are fighting
for, and exactly how right or wrong you are. In such cases, it is
rational to be stubborn, to resist, even when people of big sense
are telling you to "lighten up." In the face of injustice, and against

overwhelming odds, a little muleheadedness is more than "understandable." It is essential. The biblical character Job knew this. Whistleblowers who reveal the sins of powerful corporate executives know this. Rosa Parks on her bus in Montgomery, Alabama, knew this. So did Martin Luther King, Jr., and Gandhi and Bonhoeffer.

Liberal philosophers are not lined up to defend obstinacy, but I am learning to like stodginess and stubbornness. I do not want to try to whomp up a theory of the virtues that would logically justify these traits. I want to show why I have come to admire Dougie's stubbornness. I should warn you that I am not yet finished with his story. But I want to pause in the middle to take up another one. It concerns my grandma, an Iowan from cradle to grave.

Magda Halsor Pippert was a typical woman of little sense: loving, sensitive, godly. When there was sickness in a family, Grandma was there with dinner: scalloped potatoes, ham, fresh rhubarb pie. And yet Grandma had a backbone coveted by every Norwegian in Cerro Gordo county. Saved out of the Lutheran church (as she put it) at age twenty-one, she became a lifelong member of the Christian and Missionary Alliance, a denomination known for its courageous evangelistic forays into what was known as deepest dark Africa. My grandma spent her life caring for people, primarily her seven sons and daughters, uncountable grandchildren, husband Harry, the ladies in the church prayer circle. And she had to battle intimidating foes in her time. Trying to start out as young farmers in the 1920s, she and Harry were unable to make ends meet. They pulled up stakes and moved to California. But the cheap, fertile land they were promised turned out to be dry and expensive. In two years they were back home. They arrived, penniless and discouraged, just in time for the Depression.

Grandma had to battle not only financial woes, but spiritual opponents. One night she saw an angel at the foot of her bed. The apparition instructed her to go to mainland China as a missionary. Grandma was never able to obey. She had one son become an ordained Methodist minister, a daughter marry a C. and M. A. pastor, and her firstborn, Lois, become a missionary to Colombia. But Grandma never made it overseas for her Lord. Her inability to obey weighed heavily upon her.

She was far from being inactive spiritually. Hearing of the evils of drink from the pulpit, she became a founding member of the Iowa Women's Christian Temperance Union. This was when prohibition was a national joke. Learning of the dangers of communism from traveling evangelists, she spent hours each day praying for the triumph of Christ. And, reading of the risks of gambling, she spoke to countless Ladies' Meetings about the teachings of Scripture on greed.

She would have died had she known that Wesley and Harold attended Ritchie Valens' last concert at the Surf Ballroom in Clear Lake. Grandma fought all the temptations of the flesh, including drink, cards, movies, communism, and dancing, as well as rock 'n' roll. I take my five-year-old daughter to see the movie *La Bamba* without ever thinking how this would have appeared to her. I drink beer on Friday afternoons at DaVinci's with my students in Religious Ethics, never pausing to consider how incongruous this would seem to her. I do research on issues of economic justice in agricultural biotechnology using funds taken from the Iowa state lottery, never thinking that she would see grave irony in using gambling profits to talk about fairness in distributing wealth.

My mother's mother fought alcoholism, sexual promiscuity, paganism, and the Russians. I do not know whether she ever met an alcoholic, a prostitute, an atheist, or a Marxist. But even if the enemies she perceived are not the ones I see today, her battles are not diminished. When it comes to spiritual battles, the only real foes are the ones that appear to you.

Grandma understood Satan to be a winged fallen angel. I understand him a little closer to home, as the self in its constant attempts to become god, autonomous center of the universe. Career aspirations play an important role in many of our lives, and I often wonder about my intentions. Does a nonfarming academic write to defend family farms because he is genuinely concerned about economic justice? Or does he do it because he has had luck getting papers published in this area, and he knows that that looks good to tenure committees?

I write this particular paragraph seated at a richly stained Queen Anne desk in the Brownstone Inn at Duke University. The sun, a blazing peach bowl outside my window, sets behind the Carolinian pines. I have just come from a brisk, solitary swim in the hotel pool, a soak in its attached Jacuzzi, topped off with a frothy shower with "French milled soap, made exclusively for the Brownstone Inn." They also provide you with that deliciously scented almond shampoo that comes in a single half-ounce portion in a non-biodegradable plastic bottle. When I am tired of writing I will take the elevator to the dining room, where I will have a drink with a group of campus ministers before sitting down to prime rib and red wine.

It is with great irony that I write, as I write to defend little Christian sects like the Mennonites and Amish, family farms and small-scale economies, underprivileged women and children. There is no logical contradiction, of course; the scholarly life has always been one of a special, leisured class. Indeed, it is a necessary condition for being a thinker that one live in a luxurious society; without time free from physical labor, one literally cannot pick up a book and read or a pen and write.

There is nothing logically contradictory in what I do. But there is something pragmatically contradictory about it, and we must cultivate this little sense of uneasiness; it runs down the drain all too easily. My colleagues Joe Kupfer and David Roochnik have written about practical contradictions, in which we say one thing while doing another. It is a practical contradiction to say that you do not care about anyone. Your very act of saying it shows that you very clearly *do* care. You care enough to try to convince your listener about your carelessness. It is a practical, if not a logical, contradiction to write, "Family farms ought to be saved insofar as they treat animals more humanely than corporate farms," and then to go eat veal from small North Carolina farms. It is a practical contradiction to defend the rights of farmland hard after emptying the minuscule contents of a shampoo bottle that will never break down in the environment. It is a practical contradiction to defend the truth of the Christian doctrine of humility (*kenosis*: the emptying of God) while filling oneself with beef raised on destroyed rain forests in Brazil.

I sense the contradiction deeply. Grandma believed that Christ was among us, in our weaknesses. She tried to live a life that did not practically contradict her beliefs. I do not know whether that is possible any more. Christians drive alone in cars that waste unrenewable fuels, spray Pam on their pans releasing ozone-destroying chlorofluorocarbons, eat meals that waste calories by turning grains into meats, defecate in woefully inefficient toilets, neglect their children to secure their careers. Is it possible any more to be Christian without engaging in practical contradictions? I do not know. The only apparent answer for me is to try to separate myself—to one degree or another—from the institutions and arrangements that contradict our convictions. One way to figure out how to do this is to identify the real places—the little places—in which we actually live and move and have our being. Then, we can start clinging obstinately to the memories that hang on, and the hopes that spring up, in these specific crannies.

In the farmhouse she and Harry bought in 1939 Grandma kept a scrapbook. It was under the bed in the south room; I know because I once found it by accident. I was not looking for it; I was looking for Uncle Harold's John Deere tractor, the one with the front tires that turned when you twisted the green steering wheel. But when I was older, I went through it. I found all sorts of news clippings from the *Mason City Globe-Gazette*. Some were recent, some were ragged. They included announcements of the time and place of a weekly series of evangelistic meetings by a Brother Lawrence of the Nazarene church, a story about the furlough of a C. and M. A. missionary couple recently returned from Sierra Leone, and dozens of clippings from a daily feature in the paper offering inspirational verses from the Book of Proverbs.

On the front cover, Grandma had glued a piece of paper that read, "Watch and Pray." If people had mottoes, this would have been hers. She watched and prayed all the time, watching for the Second Coming and praying for the perishing. But she also was concerned with the powers pulling her babies away from farm country, farm life, and good Christian living. The idea of so running your farm that you would put other folk off theirs infuriated her, and on occasion she prayed about this too.

Why? Because the good Lord put us here to support, nurture, and care for one another, not to eat each other up in mad competition. She prayed on and off, silently, all day long. She prayed, out loud, in the morning and evening and before meals. Early in the day was her most productive period of meditation, from 5 A.M. until 6:30 or 7:00. She would get up alone and warm a cup of milk on the stove. Then, wrapping herself in a blanket, she would steal off to her special place in the grove. There between the chicken coop and the corn bins she would intercede on behalf of each of the children: Paul, Lois, Chuck, Marie, Wesley, Harriet, Harold. She would name each of her grandchildren, twenty and more, naming her specific joys and fears for each one. She would then get on to neighbors and friends.

She took most of her inspiration directly from her Bible, but she would also read a devotional booklet called "Our Daily Bread." Mailed every three months from the Radio Bible Class in Grand Rapids, Michigan, the booklet featured a Scripture reference at the top of each page. This would be followed by a catchy, if occasionally ungrammatical, title like "One Drink Is One Too Much." Under this she would find a verse, such as "Wine is a mocker . . . and whoever is led astray by it is not wise. Proverbs 20:1." A brief story would follow, perhaps about a missionary like John G. Paton, who once visited a businessman for dinner. Noticing his host taking a drink of whiskey, Paton asked him what on earth he was doing. "Oh," said the businessman, "my doctor prescribed it for a medical ailment. I've been doing it for eight years." Paton replied, not unseverely, that if he had been taking that kind of "medicine" for that length of time, he would stop immediately, and find a new doctor.

This would be followed by a stern warning from the narrator, "P.R.V.," who might compare drink to a boa constrictor. "That's the way it is with alcohol; the 'social drink' can be the first coil around the person. Eventually he is helpless in its grasp." Grandma would not notice the paternalistic tone or patriarchal rhetoric. Her eyes would follow on down to a brief poem, usually written by "Anon." but in this case by "D.J.D.":

> Be not a slave to alcohol,
>   Yield not to its control,
> But trust instead the grace of God,
>   To calm your heart and soul.

The bottom of the page would offer a catchy saying, like "Many things can be preserved in alcohol, but Christian character is not one of them." The moral of the tale could very well have been any one of the dozens found throughout the booklet: "Where one goes hereafter depends on what he goes after here," or "You can turn any care into prayer anywhere," or "God's salvation takes into account the LOST, the LAST, and the LEAST." Once, with an uncharacteristically irreverent wink, Grandma whispered to me that all the stories and lessons were interchangeable.

She would read slowly, meditating, using a flashlight if the winter sun were late. She would have liked the lesson about drink in particular; it was the kind to get your spiritual battery charged. And yet alcohol was not at the top of her list of demons. Drinking got into Grandma's prayers only if the particular burdens and triumphs of her offspring happened to be light that day; the burdens of Paul and Wes and Marie were her primary concerns. I suspect that she also battled her own pride. The diaries of the saints show that their biggest temptation was to try to justify themselves in their own eyes, to think that their own story about the world was the only possible one. The struggle, Grandma once said, is to learn how to think of your own little story as just one part of God's big one. I have often wondered what she meant. Did she mean that we must acknowledge the incompleteness, the unjustifiability, of our lives? It is not comforting to think that the things we do and suffer are random. It is not easy to think that I cannot write my own ticket.

Grandma's places of little sense—her kitchen, her spot in the grove, her Sunday school classroom—all these places bore her up. Her hours of prayer each morning gave her an inner strength that the male patriarchs of the church could not have matched. In the face of doubts and fears that we nonprayers can only guess at, she held firm. She was a strong woman, a shade conservative, a little obstinate. I loved her.

Because I loved her, her obstinacy always interested me. I did not fully understand it until I read an article by C. S. Lewis. Lewis pointed out that obstinacy is fully justified when its basis is experience. Rosa Parks saw the humanity of black folk. She knew that she was entitled to sit in the front of the bus, even if she could not give an extended argument about the philosophical bases of human rights. The whistleblower at the Nuclear Services Corporation saw the data on the safety of nuclear power plants. He knew that he must obstinately refuse to ignore it, even in the face of almost certain recrimination from powerful industry officials. The husband who knows his wife knows the facts. He is justified in obstinately refusing to put her to some unmotivated test of fidelity. Indeed, he is not acting rationally if he sets out to test her the moment some stranger invites him to do so. The very act of capitulating to the request may initiate problems. As Shakespeare shows in *Othello*, agreeing to test one's mate can be the first step in a chain of events that ends in the suspicion that destroys relationships. When personal experience is our foundation, obstinacy in one's beliefs is a virtue. Grandma would have agreed, adding her two cents to Lewis' theological argument: if you have met God in the grove, then you need no other reason to believe.

That said, we must also admit that stubbornness can have its price, and it is too often coupled with a lack of self-knowledge. This leads to provincialism and prejudice, which are no more forgivable for being unconscious. The answer is to season your backbone with doses of good humor.

When she was very old, a grown-up Gordie teased her.

"Grandma, speak some Norhooskie for us," he would implore her.

"Oh, Gordon. You speak some for us," she would reply.

"OK. Heineken, Lowenbrau," he would laugh, stomping on the first syllable.

Grandma did not know that these were names of different brands of beer. She watched television, and might have seen a commercial featuring athletes imbibing after the big game, but mostly she watched Billy Graham and Oral Roberts. Even if some beer advertisement had sneaked between the sheets of one of these services, she would have unconsciously tuned it out. There is no way she could have known what Lowenbrau signified.

She did know that she was being mocked. In earlier days, she might have reacted indignantly, overcome by the impertinence of her grandson. But now she would only nod her head, twinkle her eyes, frown at Gordie. She was wise enough to know not that Heineken was a beer, but that her considerable knowledge of the world was limited, and that others could sometimes see its limits. Why did this not bother her? Probably because she knew herself and could laugh at what she saw. That may have come from long years of experience watching things grow and die and turn to earth and sprout again. It may have come from a lifetime of service in which she had learned that force is overcome not with force but with little winks and nods, with holding hands with the dying, with little stories about our weaknesses. Whatever the explanation, she was a wonderfully obstinate and wise woman when she finally passed away in 1982.

Dougie, too, had the virtue needed to keep pigheadedness under control. And now I want to finish the story begun earlier. After refusing to grab his ankles and weathering my father's storm, he caught his breath back in the moving Chevy. The little Goliath-slayer turned to me.

"Gary?" he whispered, peering forward to see whether Dad could hear him.

I responded, still awed by what I had seen. "Yes?"

He looked deep into my eyes, and uttered words I will never forget. He said, "Where's my ankles?"

He was too young to be playing. The truth was that he did not know the difference between his knees and thighs and ankles, or at least under the pressure of the moment, had momentarily forgotten. I bravely volunteered this information to Mother. She immediately broke out in a huge grin. Soon Dad was laughing, and then a very puzzled Doug was laughing, and then we were all laughing and slapping each other.

What happened in that car was a testament to the demystifying power of a little sense. Doug's honesty and Mom's good humor, coupled with Dad's good nature, had worked a miracle. Where Gordie and I had destroyed the peace, and where my father's attempt at punishment had not come close to restoring it, Doug's weakness, his suffering presence, had accomplished the feat. It turned out that he had not slain the Goliath we thought he had. But, by confessing his ignorance, he had slain one.

What happened in the car is also a testament to the fragile nature of perception. We all thought we had experienced our coming-of-age; we were ready to leap to Dougie's defense. But it turned out that we had not seen what we thought we had seen. We had not seen stunning bravado; we had seen simple ignorance. I must admit that Dougie's story, charming as it is on the surface, has occasionally kept me up at night. Personal experience seems less reliable to me these days; obstinacy based on personal experience seems less pure.

Stories are funny things; they can stand you up and knock you down, and sometimes one right after the other. I first learned of this ambivalent, terrifying, potential of stories from my grandma. One of my earliest memories is of her rocking us to sleep by the clanging wall heater in the front room. The slim gray electric box must have been the pride of some mechanical engineer's eye once upon a time. But years of use had it banging and popping all night long, more conspicuous when it was quiet than when it was rumbling. Before Grandma went up to read her Bible and pray with Grandpa, before they would join hands to sleep, before they mur-

mured together their final benediction, "Come quickly, Lord Jesus," Grandma would serenade her suburban Chicago babies. Her bedtime song was surprisingly sober, an unsettling narrative set to the tune of an ancient Norwegian dirge:

Johnny and Billy went strolling one day,
Down by the clear water side,
One went up to the boatman and said,
"Please row me over the tide."

Row me over the tide,
Row me over the tide,
Loved ones are waiting for me over there,
Please row me over the tide.

Once she had worked her way into the third verse, we felt ourselves wavering. There was the boatman, waiting, there the dark lights. The cold unknown waters beckoned; pulled toward the shadows, we hesitated between Grandma and the man she seemed to push us toward. I remember the sensation fuzzily at best, but it was something like losing consciousness, as if you were a baptismal candidate having hands laid on you and being instructed to surrender to the water, trusting in a power you could not know, giving yourself—in the exact words of the rite—to death. The boatman, goes the refrain, will row you over.

Frederic Jameson has described the experience exactly. In "On Magic Realism in Film" he writes of the "shock of entry" into a story, describing the process as "the body's tentative immersion into an unfamiliar element, with all the subliminal anxieties of such submersion: the half-articulated fear of what the surface of the liquid conceals, a sense of our vulnerability along with the archaic horror of impure contact with the unclean; the anticipation of fatigue . . . the deep ambivalence at the dawning sacrifice of the self to the narrative text." Stories, far from being untrue fictions, crack our minds open, making it possible for us to get into position where the truth can be known. This is shocking, because our ordinary experience is self-deceived, closed to the fact that we must die to be born again.

People in Illinois and people in Iowa know the ambivalence and power of stories. They know that the storyteller can shake us, causing our ordinary world to look very different. Perhaps it is a sign of cowardice that we always want storytellers to get to the "point." Perhaps insisting that every story have a lesson is one way of refusing to face the boatman, of avoiding our fears about the shadowy kingdom below the surface of consciousness. Perhaps it is a way to continue the pretense that the everyday world is stable, rational, controllable. Of course, this is pretense; the real world is impure, unclean, and ultimately it devours brains and bellies both.

Many religions tell us that to gain our lives we must lose them; to understand the world we must give up our pretension to be its master or mistress; truly to know ourselves we must take leave of our senses. This is what places of big sense refuse to do; they do not encourage us to dwell in stories. Nor do stories dwell comfortably there; who has time while they are writing books and becoming famous?

Localized memories like those of my brother and grandma can help us to resist. They can teach us right obstinacy and right meekness. For things are not what they seem; the world is not predictable, we are not its Narrator, and human behavior is not run by a single true morality or economic efficiency. Stories remind us that we live in places of little sense, that the fragile plots in which we are enmeshed are deeply ironic. We live amidst funny, terrifying paradoxes, in which our most unbending heroes may simply not know where to find their ankles. And yet the screw is always turning one more time: our unmasked heroes turn out, in the end, to have slain the most ferocious of dragons.

I recently visited my grandma's grave in Nora Springs. My mother met me, having driven from Wheaton. She stooped to remove twigs from the headstone, wondering aloud when Harold had been here last. I did not answer, knowing that she could see it had not been long: the geranium box had been moved. Somehow, I remember thinking, this place pulls at me, tugging me toward its dark lights. I do not like cemeteries, and thinking of Grandma's backbone, now a fine gray mound of dust in the casket, is not cheering. Yet somehow it upholds me, giving me direction. And it bears down upon me, making its claim, insisting that I explain my life. I have not succeeded in doing that; I cannot remember all of the multifarious details, or fashion the ones I do remember into a coherent plot. But I can remember some things, and what I remember I can retell.

Isn't that, Mom, the best we can do?

JANET KAUFFMAN

Letting Go: The Virtue
of Vacant Ground

D rive around southern Michigan these days, and
you'll see the new look of farmland. It's wild.
Unkempt. Downright gorgeous.

Where, in the past, you'd have seen a regimen of rows, now you
see weedy sprawl. Where there were singular crops, there's a riot
of undergrowth, wind-seeded. There is raggedness, mess, variety,
mix. On its own, out of human control, farmland demonstrates an
abundance—flourishing, bizarre, rank, twisted, vital. And the
feel, in a way, is more urban than rural: boom and surprise and
decay, all in one.

With the farm economy aggravated by grain surpluses, with
corn and bean prices in steep decline, it's not unusual in southern
Michigan to see a countryside visibly changed by the abandonment of farms, or the abandonment of traditional field practices. A
lot of places around here, everything's gone to seed. Government
set-aside programs have opened up huge spaces to cover crops;
and many farmers, on their own, have begun to let marginal fields
lie fallow—just let them go. The gravelly hills, glacial dumps,
the undrained low-lying clays—they're easy to give up now. It's
cheaper, most of the time, not to till and plant them.

If you examine any square foot of unfarmed ground—a square
foot which a few years ago would have contained some dirt and a
couple of cornstalks—you will find this: quack grass, of course,

like a mat, and milkweed, ragweed, or pigweed, lamb's-quarters, maybe some bergamot. Weeds. All weeds. Nothing planted, nothing for profit. Nobody cultivates weeds. But in this economy—here is the virtue, to start—they cost the farmer nothing.

The virtues that follow, and accumulate, are more crucial, more enticing, in the long run; but the fact that weeds are cost-efficient—no production costs, no harvest costs—is good enough to begin with. Farmers here, a few, have learned how to tolerate the velvetleaf or goldenrod, rampant in a vacant field, and have figured out how to see something in the scene besides trouble.

To somebody who hasn't farmed, the scenery is unambiguous, spectacular: weeds bloom in field after field of flower. This time of year, late July, the commonplace explosion of Queen Anne's lace—hand-size white bursts at the roadsides—proliferates outward, into acres of old fields. It's a painterly, splotchy wash. Although ragweed and goldenrod haven't flowered yet, they've shot up to chest height, green and feathery, so there is an expansion and bunching of foliage and vegetation, on to the horizon. In the most meager soils, chicory stalks, like stubble, appear—the flower bits of blue; and sweet clover takes over gravel slopes, a serious tangle of tough stem and small, indeterminate leaf.

Any parcel of marginal, uncultivated land breaks out in these stupendous varieties of weed, diverse but not as random as one might think. Without the inhibition of herbicides or the row arrangement of cultivation, plants emerge according to preferences for soil type, composition, elevation, moisture. By the looks of things—the colors, the textures—you can spot even slight gradations in slope, and all the shifts from sand to loam to gravel to muck.

Looking across these fields is an education in the designs of ease. In natural selection. Adaptation. Variety. In wildness. In one of the plain pleasures of human vision: seeing something not human.

Gone wild, even the first year, a field becomes a thigh-high jungle. Anybody trying to walk through these waste places understands there is no vacancy, none, in "vacant ground."

By vacant ground, we mean, of course, unfarmed, uncultivated land. Uncontrolled by us. *Not* farming marginal farmlands, letting some land go wild or lie fallow, was common farm practice, a regenerative practice, before the use of chemical fertilizers. Now, with some choice in the matter, in a redefined economy, farmers again can acknowledge the value of vacant ground, the virtue— why not call it that?—of letting go.

My concern here, the more I look around, is not agricultural but moral: a concern for how human beings use land.

Farming, like mining or house-building or any construction, is one way humans use land; it is no more "natural" a land use than oil-drilling. So I am not talking about farming as pastoral, or profitable, or good for the soul. Not at all. Farming, here, is *provocateur*—it's made me think. And what I am thinking about is how human beings inhabit the earth.

I have lived in the hummocky glacial dumping ground of southern Michigan for more than sixteen years, almost as long as I lived in the limestone-bedded and rolling farmlands of Lancaster County, Pennsylvania, where I grew up. And while Michigan isn't a wilderness, it certainly is wild, unruly, as scenery, compared to the farm landscapes I knew as a child. This part of Michigan—a good bit of it swampland when white settlers first arrived, a place notorious for mosquitoes and bad air—remains, because of the problems with drainage, and the more extreme ranges of seasons and rainfall, much less domesticated, much less rich than eastern Pennsylvania. Not many farms here have the neat arrangement of barns, with good paint, the encompassing fields and pastures, that show up on the postcards of Lancaster County.

From a Michigan point of view, though—and that's what I have now—the pastoral aura, the precision, of postcard farms looks more like tyranny than bliss.

A good Lancaster County farm had few hedgerows, very small woodlots, lawn to the barns and lawn around the barns. No weeds. Tangle was akin to sin. Land was tillable, and therefore the land was tilled. Whatever grew was planted. And always for human use. (When I moved to Michigan and first saw the huge leaves of wild burdock, I thought, good lord, *rhubarb*! The mad Germanic notion that if it was there, it had been planted, and could probably be cooked.) In Lancaster County it would have been unseemly, a serious lapse in responsibility, to let a field, even a rocky slope, grow up in weeds. The same obsession with order and control of the landscape continues there now, even though most of the farms, because they were "scenic," are gone—sold to developers, and subdivided and recut with streets of houses. Each development wanted a view of the next farm. No postcards now. But the order persists, and it follows from the same tyrannical, familiar assumption: humans have the right, the obligation, to work and rearrange, and "order" the natural world. The wild is a place to be tamed. It is an arrogant designation of priority—make the world over for humans. Americans, seeing landscape from the beginning as real estate, are scrupulous about dealing in it, and in prosperous areas all over the country, a fierce moral judgment falls on "waste" places, scrubland, even the vacant lots in developments, where the ragweed's got a good hold. For God's sake, do something with it! everybody says.

In Michigan, too, you hear remnants of a wish for control. Shreds of it. When I called my neighbor to borrow a cultipacker—the wide iron cylinder that would press down the seeds of a new prairie patch—her question about the coneflowers and partridge pea, predictably, was, "So, will the stuff spread?" She knew it would. And her question carried the comic knowingness—the willful resignation—that comes with living where human control isn't absolute. Where weeds win.

There's a kind of what-the-hell feel to farming here. You do what you can, but the uneven ground, the clay pockets, the swamps—they're a powerful opposition. You compromise. You give in. Sometimes, you just let go. You can't delude yourself into thinking that farming is God's work, or a good man or woman's work. You lose faith in the idea of beauty as a mowed yard. You don't look at an aerial picture of your farm and think, ah, peace. Harmony.

Instead, you haul rocks. You pull out mulberry and locust trees that sprout in fields. You spray quack grass. You say, "So, will the stuff spread?" And sometimes—when it finally makes sense—you let cracked drainage tiles stay cracked. You let the swamp be a swamp. You let the locusts sprout and take over a stony field. You stop baling hay in the wet low places where the bales came in damp and molded anyway.

I've done every one of these things, and every one is a mindful struggle. Things look worse, for a while. In a way. When I stopped farming some fields, I minded the scrappiness as much as any dead-end farmer. I thought about putting up signs—Wildlife Preserve—as an excuse, an explanation. And one of these days I might get around to doing it. Not as an excuse anymore, but because it's the truth.

Taking the care (and it *is* care, not lassitude) to hang on to productive land and let go of the hills, the holes, the margins, some farmers have found it's even possible to make money. One farmer near here, who reduced his acreage to the good acreage, makes more money farming 140 acres than another farmer makes working 1,000 acres of unselected fields, farmed straight through, no matter what the lay of the land or the condition of the soil. But there is the "clean" farm, spread out. People say, oh, take a picture. We like these pictures, the photogenic. And in farming, that usually means as complete a control of natural conditions as possible.

A number of untamed, unadulterated beauties have survived in this country, singled out and preserved, protected. When the dream of wilderness confronts the dream of the tamed farm (Americans know how to split the soul), we've often done a good job saving our "natural wonders." But to be wonders, wild places must meet substantial requirements as dramatic (Yosemite), spectacularly bizarre (Yellowstone), grand (the Grand Canyon). Even if we've done fairly well preserving the dramatic and starkly beautiful, we'd also do well to attend to ordinary places, the nondramatic, waste and wayside places—all habitats and sceneries.

To a farmer, it sounds simple. We must finally recognize the rights of the earth. Civil rights, human rights, women's rights, animal rights—all these move outward, expand in implication, if we keep at it, toward the planet's rights. The human compulsion—centuries old—to use land rather than inhabit it must ultimately appear barbaric, an extreme form of domination and exploitation.

We have grown rich on tyrannical ideas: the idea that the world is a resource, full of goods, for human consumption; the idea that tillable ground should be tilled—an idea that cleared the pines, utterly, from the state of Michigan in the last century; an idea that is clearing jungles and "bringing life" to some deserts today and causing desertification elsewhere. We have an arsenal of ideas about land use possibly as dangerous to human life on the planet as the use of nuclear arms.

And worse, we have no global plan, no serious national debate, concerning the preservation of land and landscape. In fact, in the development and use of coastlines, for instance (and lakeshores, and water rights), recent court decisions persist in supporting private landowners' rights rather than the broader "public interest"—

although even that interest, too often one state's or one nation's interest, can be extremely narrow. Americans who regard as sacred the right to hold private property must also ask at some point, what are the rights of the property itself? This is not simply an environmental question, although environmentalists are the ones we most often hear from (the ones who, like Earth First protesters in the Northwest lumbering districts, are labeled "environmental guerrillas"). What are the rights of the earth itself? And another way of asking it is: how should humans inhabit a world not wholly human?

After all, this is a world of rock and water and air. It is elemental. It is not ours.

Our rights cannot be exclusive. Human habitation of the planet must be based on mutuality, not domination. Feminists know this territory. Some farmers do. If we care about the land, it will be necessary to redefine whole economies, not just the farm economy. A complex, solid economy could certainly grow around a policy of cooperation with natural environments. Why haven't we proposed such policies—on as grand a scale as national defense—when our own species is at stake?

We are primitives in our thinking about economies. We are babes. We believe the world is ours, like a heated house. Landscape is sold for holiday viewing. This culture and this economy promote the idea of all-terrain vehicles and disregard the idea of terrain. From an ATV, the landscape is backdrop, nothing more. It's scenery on an ad. You roar through it. That's it.

Almost every April, guys on three-wheelers rip through the beech woods at the back of this farm and cut down the stream bank. With the trillium and rue anemone, it's a pretty place to ride through, with enough rocks in the water for a scare. Once when my son and I caught up with the machines—there were three of them, stalled in some swamp willows, as far into scrub as they could drive—it was clear these were men prepared for combat: they had the camouflage waterproof gear, the helmets and goggles, buckled gloves.

We smugly dismiss the last century, its imperialisms and arrogances and abuses, as unenlightened. They were blind. We can see the arrogance and abuse. But in our own world, we see again, once again, progress. *Development* is one of our favorite, most blessed, words. Real estate development. Third World development. Arctic development. Development for tourism.

Instead of new housing starts (more developments, more subdivisions) as one of the measures of an economy's health, why not new reclamation starts? Why not?

After all, this is a world of rock and water and air. It is elemental. It is not ours.

What do we want to *do* with it? Because we are conscious creatures, the entire planet—the universe—has become a place for the pleasure of the human mind. And being human, we *must* range and speculate. We must terrify ourselves with our thinking. This is our art.

But in the dailiness of human life, in the physical world of carbon and hydrogen, oxygen and uranium, we may not range thoughtlessly or speculate endlessly to our gain. The world is not ours to use up, or blanket with our debris, or despoil.

In this century, we have made of the world an elaborate, grotesque, noxious cake—it's layered and layered with richness and artificial decoration: a global and decadent art, the mind can say. Who can eat it? Who wants to? What is the appetite that cooked it up, or could be satisfied by it? Set the globe in a great gallery, and it would be something to see.

But life is not art. Or rather, it *dare not* be. We dare not let it be, or the world will be lost. Lost to us, and lost to all artless things— the matter—of the earth. Some knowledge—death (which is inevitable)—cannot be lived (except through art), and therefore it must be known and accepted. Other knowledges—violence, destruction, tyranny (which is not inevitable)—cannot be lived with for long (except through art), and therefore these must be known, and rejected.

It is possible to reconceive the world. It's been done. In the past, humans changed their minds; they went from heresy to new belief. It became apparent: the Earth, the Ptolemaic center of things, was not the Galilean center. It became apparent: slavery, economically feasible, was not morally tolerable.

It must also become apparent: the physical destruction of the planet—right here, an easy mark—is a crime.

In the terror of ancient times, humans could live intimately with the natural world. Without technologies, they no doubt lived in awe. And in peril.

With our technologies—ones of incalculable power: earth-shattering, planet-altering; and ones of incredible potential: earth-restoring, planet-preserving—we can rediscover an intimacy, a mutuality with the natural world, that is not primitive (though based in part on fear), but *knowing*. It might even be possible to relearn a life of awe. And inhabit landscape without violation. With the least violation.

There will be nothing simple about living generously, coherently, and intimately with the natural world.

If I'm happy to see a few Midwest fields go wild, it's a small thing. I know. But re-viewing, re-conceiving the land we inhabit, is not a small thing. It is not nostalgia to sing the praises of vacant ground. It is not longing for the past, but an immoderate and profound desire for the future, that leads a person to say—about wasteland and wetland and any steep slope and any undeveloped shoreline—let it go. Let it be.

NOTES ON CONTRIBUTORS

DOUGLAS BAUER was raised on a central Iowa farm; his home town is the subject of his first book, *Prairie City, Iowa*. His articles, reviews, and stories have appeared in the *Atlantic, Esquire, Harper's, Epoch*, the *New York Times Magazine*, and other publications. He has taught at Drake University, Ohio State University, SUNY Albany, and most recently in the expository writing program at Harvard. He is finishing a new novel, *Dexterity*.

GARY COMSTOCK, assistant professor of philosophy and chair of the Religious Studies Program at Iowa State University, is the editor of *Is There a Moral Obligation to Save the Family Farm?* His areas of scholarly interest are philosophy of religion and agricultural ethics. He is married to Karen Werner Comstock, and they have two children, Krista and Ben.

LOUISE ERDRICH was born and grew up in Wahpeton, North Dakota. Her first two novels, *Love Medicine* and *The Beet*

Queen, will be followed this fall by another, *Tracks*. She has also published a book of poems, *Jacklight*. She lives with her husband, Michael Dorris, and their children in New Hampshire.

DAVID HAMILTON is professor of English at the University of Iowa; since 1977 he has also edited the *Iowa Review*. His essays have appeared in a variety of journals, including three previous publications sponsored by the Iowa Humanities Board.

JANET KAUFFMAN has published three books of poems, *Writing Home, The Weather Book*, and *Where the World Is*, and two books of fiction, *Places in the World a Woman Could Walk* and *Collaborators*. In 1985 she received the Rosenthal Award from the Academy-Institute of Arts and Letters. She lives in Hudson, Michigan, where she teaches and farms—less and less every year.

MICHAEL MARTONE has published two books of short

stories, *Alive and Dead in Indiana* and *Safety Patrol*. Born in Fort Wayne, Indiana, he has lived since 1980 in Story County, Iowa, where he taught writing at Iowa State University. While in Iowa he edited the magazine *Poet&Critic* and with his wife, Theresa Pappas, published a series of chapbooks called Story County Books. Currently, he writes on agricultural issues for the *North American Review* and is Briggs-Copeland Lecturer on Fiction at Harvard University.

MICHAEL J. ROSEN is the author of a book of poems, *A Drink at the Mirage*, and a children's picture book, *Fifty-Odd Jobs*. His fiction, criticism, and poetry have appeared in *Salmagundi*, *Threepenny Review*, *Prairie Schooner*, *Grand Street*, *New Criterion*, and *Southwest Review*; he has been awarded fellowships by the Ohio Arts Council, the National Endowment for the Arts, and the In-gram Merrill Foundation. He has been the literary director of the Thurber House, the writers' center in the restored Columbus home of James Thurber, since its inception in 1982.

JANE STAW has taught at Stanford University and the University of California at Berkeley. She has published poems in *Columbia*, the *Agni Review*, and the *Iowa Review*, and she is the translator of *A Day in the Strait* by the French poet Emmanuel Hocquard.

MARY SWANDER has published essays, short stories, and two books of poems, *Succession* and *Driving the Body Back*. She has received the *Nation*-Discovery Award, the Carl Sandburg Award, and two Ingram Merrill Foundation grants; in 1987 she was awarded a National Endowment for the Arts fellowship. She teaches at Iowa State University.